Startup to Success

Startup to Success
A Startup Guide for the Empowered Entrepreneur

NATASHA M PALUMBO

Eternal Enterprise Publishing

Startup to Success

Copyright © 2021 by Natasha M Palumbo. All rights reserved.

No part of this book may be reproduced or transmitted in any form or by any means, electronic or mechanical, including photocopying, recording, or by any information storage and retrieval system, without the express written permission of the author.

First Printing: 2021

ISBN-13: 978-1-7344905-4-1

Author Bio Photograph By: Juan Padilla with Luxus Photos
Book Cover Designed By: Joanne Jenkins and Natasha Palumbo with Ldy Bug Images

Eternal Enterprise Publishing
Sacramento, CA Ordering Information:
Special discounts are available on quantity purchases by corporations, associations, educators, and others. For details, contact the publisher at the address listed above.

U.S. trade bookstores and wholesalers:
Please contact Natasha M Palumbo
Email natasha@natashapalumbo.com

To my beautiful granddaughter, Nala Jhené Brown

Contents

Foreword

Acknowledgments

Note to the Reader

Introduction

Chapter 1

Self Discovery: The Key to Success 1

Chapter 2

Time and Project Management 22

Chapter 3

Human-Centered Design Thinking 36

Chapter 4

Business Legal Structure and Intellectual Property 46

Chapter 5

DBA, EIN, Bank Account, and Business Insurance 65

Chapter 6

Business Planning 79

Chapter 7

Effective Communication 91

Chapter 8

Marketing and Branding 102

Chapter 9

Networking 128

Chapter 10

The Power of Human Capital.. 140

Chapter 11

Leadership.. 148

Chapter 12

Money Management 164

Chapter 13

Accounting and Taxes... 182

Chapter 14

Revenue Model and Pricing... 169

Chapter 15

Startup Cost, Break-Even Point, and Funding Your Business............... 194

Chapter 16

The Secret to Success.. 205

Bonus Chapter

Welfare to Wealth Story.. 224

Appendicies

References and Resources

About the Author

Foreword

For those of you who are brave enough, confident enough, and lucky enough to read this book, you better get ready to highlight, take notes, and reread pages. From start to finish, *Startup to Success* is a step-by-step guide to building your successful business.

Natasha Palumbo has taken the dark tunnel of starting your own business and shone a bright light of clarity on it. If you follow this book through each step, take massive action, stay gritty and consistent, and never lose sight of your goals, success will be inevitable. I have built several companies over the last six years—all of them have failed but one. These failures have taught me invaluable lessons, lessons that I could have learned sooner through books like this one.

Though my latest company has gone from $0–80k+ a month in 18 months, I had to make many tweaks to allow my profit to go from a measly 5–15% to a healthy 50–60%. I adjusted the culture and processes of my company to better serve my clients. I established strategic partnerships that has over 500x'd my lead generation, while working less hours. I built relationships that have taken my life to a whole different level in every capacity. Also, did I mention I'm twenty-five?

What was the difference between my first startup that failed miserably and my most recent successful business? A successful business does not start with an LLC, business cards, and a website. It starts with your mindset. The six inches between your ears will define your success in anything you do. Nothing pulls more weight in building a successful life than your mindset. Like Jim Rohn said, *"Learn to work harder on yourself than you do on your job. If you work hard on your job you can make a living, but if you work hard on yourself you'll make a fortune."* Building the skills of focus, grit, and mastering the art of positive thinking will pay greater dividends than sleek business cards. *Startup to Success* teaches you everything you will need to know to get your mindset right. Then, with that proper mindset, you will learn how to put this new you to work!

Sales is the life blood for the everyday startup. Without sales, there is no business. A positive mental attitude is imperative, but it will not pay your bills. You must also put in the work. You must obsess over the client experience, lead generation and conversion, and money management. These three pillars will drive your sales through the roof. CEOs have many jobs. However, most important are those three things. Every day you must be working on them. This is what I did with my company and it has allowed me to see explosive growth. Each alone is not enough, but all three will take any company to any level you desire.

When broken down into simple steps that are followed deliberately and executed at a high level, you can start to see how your startup will be successful. Too many people become entrepreneurs thinking that it's easy to become successful. There's a reason why they are called the 1 percent. Most people are not willing to make the sacrifices necessary to stay consistent long enough. Be willing to admit you're wrong. Learn to adjust, to change, and to adapt to new information. Check your ego at the door, take a deep breath, and realize that success is not a destination. It is a journey and a process.

You've already taken the first step because you are holding your toolbox, your navigational system to guide you and to help you overcome any challenges that come your way. Let *Startup to Success* guide you in creating your successful business! Good luck, and I'm looking forward to seeing you next to me on the cover of *Forbes* one day!

—Henry Eisenstein, Owner of the Real Estate Enhanced Team

Acknowledgments

Father God, I thank You for the beautiful gift of life, Your eternal love, and amazing grace. Without You, I am nothing. But through You, I am Natasha M Palumbo, the daughter of the Most High. All honor and glory to Your name.

Thank you to my incredible children and amazing daughter-in-love for being with me on this journey. Allan, you inspire me in more ways than you could even begin to imagine. It is because of you that I have life today. I am so proud of the man you have become and are growing into. Thank you for always encouraging me with your youthful wisdom and joyful humor. I treasure our relationship. Brianna, I couldn't have asked for a better daughter-in-love. You are a beautiful soul with a strength that is supernatural. Your story is meant to be shared with this world, just as mine is. I encourage you in your voice. In your power. Annabella, thank you for sharing your heart with me, and for being so patient while I work and build the empire. I firmly believe you will be a writer too, and one day your writings will appear where mine leave off. You will always be protected by your brother, who will never lead you astray. I love you all so very much. Thank you for loving me with an eternal love. Remember, love is the only thing that is real. Everything else is an illusion.

Thank you to my best friend, Joanne Jenkins. I have written this before, but it still stands true today. You are more than a best friend; you are my sister. You help keep me sane and silly all in the same beat. We are the better solution! I love you.

Thank you to all my students and those whom I have had the honor of teaching. I write and speak my truth so that you may be inspired and gain greater knowledge. That you may be set free from the many matrices of this life. You all mean so much to me. Thank you for being with me on this journey and giving me a purpose to write for.

Note to the Reader

Dear reader, I want to thank you for your support. The fact that you are reading this book tells me that you are ready to be an empowered entrepreneur. You will find a wealth of information in these pages. *Startup to Success* is full of up-to-date tools, strategies, and resources that will help you in life and in business.

I am in the business of building up people who build businesses. I am honored to be able to help you build, too. You may visit my website at the address listed below. There, you will find all the services and products I offer. I am a business adjunct professor for several colleges in the state of California, as well as a coach and consultant. I have been an entrepreneur since 2002. I am passionate about business and education. In addition to teaching, I host several workshops in the California area and online. I firmly believe that we can and should live an *EMPOWERED* life. I would love for you to connect with me. You can find me on LinkedIn and Instagram @ Natasha M Palumbo.

Be well,
Natasha M Palumbo, MBA

Author, Coach, Consultant, and Speaker
Entrepreneur – Educator – Empowered
www.natashapalumbo.com

INTRODUCTION

Welcome to *Startup to Success,* an empowered entrepreneur's startup guide. I don't know about you, but I have found that most startup guides are geared more toward high-tech startups and not the everyday small businesses. But there are more startups that are non-tech. Therefore, I created this guide/workbook for those who are interested in doing uncommon, extraordinary things outside of the tech industry.

Allow me to introduce myself. My name is Natasha M Palumbo, also known as Professor Palumbo. I have the privilege and honor of working with students of all ages, not only in the colleges where I teach, but also in the entrepreneurial and empowerment workshops I facilitate. In addition, I consult with small business owners, many of whom are just starting up. My specialty is minority- and female-owned businesses. I do not take the calling of being an educator and consultant lightly. I understand that I am accountable to those I serve, and that they must be ready if they have appeared.

"When the student is ready, the teacher will appear."
—Lao Tzu

In the back of this book, I have shared my welfare to wealth story. Make sure you read it. I recommend you read it before you start chapter 1. I hope it gives you encouragement for your entrepreneurial journey. Remember, it is a marathon, not a sprint. Make sure to pace yourself and stop along the way to breathe. Far too often, I see entrepreneurs work themselves to the bone. I am not one to knock working, but I have learned that being excessive is never good. Balance is key. This is not to say you will not work much harder than most, because in order to really be in this game, you will. You must. But you will also need to learn the mastery of meditation and take the medicine of breath. By doing so, your ability to execute will skyrocket. And execution is vital. You can do all the planning you'd like, but if you do not execute, you have nothing.

There are a total of sixteen chapters in this book, fifteen of which are interactive. Self-discovery is key to going from startup to success in your business and in your life. Therefore, we are starting there. You will learn to master time and no longer allow time to master you. Because mastering time is so important to your journey, you will see that it will come directly after self-discovery. I will also be sharing with you how to do project management. You will need to understand how to move a project through from start to finish. This skill set will be critical to your startup. Then, we are going to move forward and learn about human-centered design thinking and the role it plays in the startup world. Moving right along, we will shift into the land of business legal structures and intellectual property, after which we will jump into business planning and, most importantly, the business model canvas, which is one of the most widely used tools in the startup world. I will share other important aspects of business planning, including the feasibility study and the power of your pitch deck. Please keep in mind that business plans, no matter what level, are living, breathing documents.

Continuing our journey, we will dive deeply into marketing and branding—both of which are some of my favorite topics to cover. After that, we will travel into networking and the power of human capital. We will also be working with money. Just as you will learn to master your time so it no longer masters you, you will also learn the discipline of money management and how to properly fund your startup so it succeeds. Finally, we will end with The Secret to Success, where I will give you keys and tips that are sure to help you move from startup to success and, more importantly, be empowered!

It is time for us now to turn our attention to self-discovery. You are going to do some deep diving into yourself, and I will introduce you to the jungle, where you will meet the four animals that reside in all of us. I will also have you take a grit test to see what your level of grit is at. You must be gritty in order to succeed in the startup game. You are going to write out your "why" statement, do some goal setting, and create a vision board for your business. Yes, you read that correctly. A vision board is a powerful tool. I have them everywhere. There is power in vision. You are going to channel what you desire to see for your business. Shall we begin?

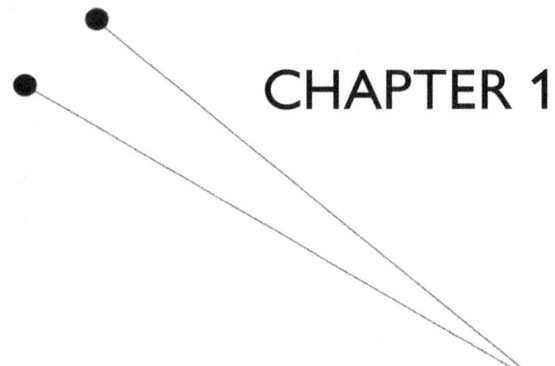

CHAPTER 1

Self-Discovery: The Key to Success

"Once your mindset changes, everything on the outside will change along with it."

—Steve Maraboli, author

The mind of an empowered entrepreneur is much different than the average mind. We think very differently. Sure, we have similar characteristics—and I even provide you with several of them in my book—but it is the mind that makes you not only an empowered entrepreneur, but also an empowered individual. We have a growth mindset, an entrepreneurial mindset, which is one that sees opportunity when others see roadblocks. One that knows with hard work and dedication, no matter how many times I fail or fall on my face, I will rise again. We understand that we have the power to create our future; we do not predict it. We understand that we don't need to control the future because, by doing so, we only create stress. We understand the power of the mind. We know that what we create will come to pass if we faint not. Chapter 1 is dedicated to personal self-discovery. You are going to go through a series of activities that ask you to take a good look at your mind. You are going to need to be honest with your answers because that is the only way you can grow. We are always growing. We never arrive, you understand—never. Personal growth should be pursued unto death. Meaning, you are in the long game. This is a marathon, not a sprint. There really is no finish line. Old ceilings become new floors. Are you ready to be EMPOWERED? If so, let's begin.

"The way out is within."

—Natasha M Palumbo

Self-awareness is key to living the EMPOWERED life. You must understand the inner man and work on the inner self in order for your "outer world" to be a true reflection of what you desire. The world we live in is a jungle—you either eat or get eaten. It is up to you. I am a LION. But I am not only a LION, I'm also a flamingo, a chameleon, and a turtle. I use all four of my animals to their full capacity. I'm in constant pursuit of personal development. Lao Tzu said, "Knowing others is wisdom, knowing yourself is Enlightenment." I need to know if you are ready to be enlightened. You will use many tools along the way to get there. I am going to share three that I believe are some of the most important. I call it the "ALL." A stands for your animal. I will introduce you to the four animals in just a bit. The first L stands for Learning style. Do you know your learning style? Knowing how you learn is so important. We often lead in the same way we learn. But not everyone learns like us. As an educator, I make sure I do my best to teach others their learning style. I have all my students take a VARK survey to indicate which learning style is their most predominant. From this survey, I can build a stronger educational portal for them that is catered to their needs. My learning style is kinesthetic and visual. I have to put my hands on it. I need to see it. Reading a handbook will not do it for me. Knowing your learning style will benefit you now and in the future as you build your startup to success. I will provide you with the link to the VARK survey, and I want you to find out what your learning style is.

Finally, the last L stands for LOVE. At our core, we desire to be loved and to love. You see, love is the only thing that is real. Everything else is an illusion. Love never dies but it does transcend, as each of us will do one day. Do you know what your love language is? Well, guess what? I'm going to provide a website where you can take a quick survey to find out. My love language is words. I can be absolutely intoxicated with words and not have one drink! I also need some quality time to make me feel loved. When we know our love language, we can communicate it to those we love, and when we find out what theirs is, we can better love them. Oh, what a world it would be if we had all these keys. Well, you're going to have them now! And how do you change the world? You start with yourself.

I would like to introduce you to the four animals now. This concept comes from the 4 Animals Assessment created by Chris Daniel.[1] First, there is a lion, and you have already read that I am a lion. We run this jungle. At least we think we do. We are results driven. Did you know that a lion is only awake four hours out the day? However, what they get done in those four hours is enough to let everyone in the jungle know they are in charge. The same is true with human lions. We execute at a very high level. What it takes someone else to do in an eight-hour day we finish in four hours.

The next animal I would like for you to meet is the very flashy, ever so beautiful, never shuts up, and doesn't like to be alone, flamingo. They are the hostess with the mostest. They will make anyone feel right at home. Very social, the flamingo's strength is by far its ability to communicate, but they can go for long periods of time if not constrained. They make some of the best conversationalists, and you are sure to enjoy the company of a flamingo. Next, I would like to introduce you to the chameleon. What is the first thing that comes to mind when you think of a chameleon? One of the first things most people think of is adaptability, or the ability to change color and blend in. Indeed, the chameleon is one of the best supporters around because they will adapt to their environment. That is, until they feel the need to go support someone else. Then they can be called shady—no pun intended. Many times, chameleons are suffering in silence. They struggle with making a decision. They don't want to hurt anyone, but oftentimes they end up hurting themselves. They can feel torn and be pulled at from too many directions. This can make it hard for them to function. They simply want to see that everyone makes it to shore safely.

The fourth and final animal I would like to introduce you to is the turtle. Everyone needs a turtle on their team. They are the ones with the details. They are going to be cautious and careful with just about everything. However, they can get in their own way trying to get everything in order. They are slow to execute because they are carefully checking things out from all angles. They are the ones who need all the details, and then they need just a bit more. They are big on systems and are wonderful planners. However, if something doesn't go to plan, they can be thrown off.

These are your four animals, and each one of them resides in us. We each have them but at varying levels. My most dominate animal is the lion, but coming in at a close second is my flamingo. I have very little chameleon and almost no turtle, which always cracks me up because I swear I'm a details person and I care for everyone—I do. But then there comes a point where we just have to go, regardless if all the pieces are in place or people are ready. Work must be done, and I am expecting to see results.

It is my lion that has saved me time and time again due to my intense and tragic backstory. I could not have grown my business the way I did without my lion. I can attest that I move quickly and need to hurry up and slow down. I need to activate turtle power and pull out more details. I need to slow down and wait a few moments longer, then attack. I have never been big on assessments because I'm an anomaly and I just can't be put into a box, but the 4 Animals is a much different assessment. It tells you your natural side and your adaptable side. We change depending on where we are. I am very fascinated by the way we adapt. Reason being is I hide. I used to hide a lot. I was hiding because I had been abused for so long that I had no true confidence in the beauty of my authentic self. It was not until I began to do the work required to heal myself that I started to love myself. It took a lot of work to get where I am today, and I'm still working on my healing because I refuse to die with the demons. In this life, you must do the work to heal yourself. I believe in personal development and growth. The 4 Animals Assessment is a tool I used along my journey, and now I share it in all my workshops, classes, and, of course, I write about it.

The four animals are the strength in my superpowers. I'm learning to master each of them to make me a better leader, educator, servant, friend, and parent. I encourage you to take the assessment, which only takes about five minutes. You get a full report that is extremely valuable, especially in regard to building your resume or biography. The report consists of in-depth information regarding how to communicate effectively with others and how you like to be communicated with. This is golden. Just like finding out what your love language is, finding out how you communicate and how you prefer to be spoken to is vital to living a more empowered life. If you would like to learn more about the assessment, you can find more information on my website or you may contact me directly. Remember, the way out is within. The deeper you crawl within and heal, the freer you will become. Life is short. How much time has already been lost? Too much, I say—and that ends now.

Now I want you to move forward with the self-awareness activity. Below are website links to the VARK survey and the love language quiz. Take them and get your results. Be sure to make note of what they are and spend some time reflecting on what you discovered. I also want you to take a guess at what you think your most dominant animal is. If and when you get to take the assessment, it will be fun to see how well you matched up.

https://vark-learn.com/the-vark-questionnaire/[2]

https://www.5lovelanguages.com/quizzes/³

I also want you to think about the following questions: Are you a morning person, afternoon, or night? Your energy level: When do you work best? Spend some time on how you handle constructive feedback. Are you a people-pleaser? How well are you dealing with others? Do you get along with people, or is there always some type of issue when dealing with others? After you have answered all those questions, I want you to answer these following three questions:

1. What do you want from and/or for your life?

2. What are you willing to start and stop in order to get what you want from and/or for your life?

3. Who is counting on you? (You counting on you counts too.)

Space to write and reflect:

_____
_____
_____
_____
_____
_____
_____
_____
_____
_____
_____
_____
_____

Grit Test

The dice of life will toss you a "no" time and time again. I need you to pick up those dice and shake them, spit on them if you must, and throw them back to this world and say, "My 'YES' is UNDENIABLE!" Grit is passion and perseverance over a long period of time in pursuit of your goals. You need to understand that in order to go from startup to success, you must be gritty. Below, you will find a grit test. I want you to take the test and see how gritty you are. If you score low, do not worry. You can grow stronger, and you will.

12-Item Grit Scale

Directions for taking the Grit Scale: Please respond to the following items. Be honest. There are no right or wrong answers!

1. I have overcome setbacks to conquer an important challenge.
    a. Very much like me
    b. Mostly like me
    c. Somewhat like me
    d. Not much like me
    e. Not like me at all
2. New ideas and projects sometimes distract me from previous ones.
    a. Very much like me
    b. Mostly like me
    c. Somewhat like me
    d. Not much like me
    e. Not like me at all
3. My interests change from year to year.
    a. Very much like me
    b. Mostly like me
    c. Somewhat like me
    d. Not much like me
    e. Not like me at all
4. Setbacks don't discourage me.
    a. Very much like me

b. Mostly like me

c. Somewhat like me

d. Not much like me

e. Not like me at all

5. I have been obsessed with a certain idea or project for a short time but later lost interest.*

   a. Very much like me

   b. Mostly like me

   c. Somewhat like me

   d. Not much like me

   e. Not like me at all

6. I am a hard worker.

   a. Very much like me

   b. Mostly like me

   c. Somewhat like me

   d. Not much like me

   e. Not like me at all

7. I often set a goal but later choose to pursue a different one.

   a. Very much like me

   b. Mostly like me

   c. Somewhat like me

   d. Not much like me

   e. Not like me at all

8. I have difficulty maintaining my focus on projects that take more than a few months to complete.

   a. Very much like me

   b. Mostly like me

   c. Somewhat like me

   d. Not much like me

   e. Not like me at all

9. I finish whatever I begin.
    a. Very much like me
    b. Mostly like me
    c. Somewhat like me
    d. Not much like me
    e. Not like me at all
10. I have achieved a goal that took years of work.
    f. Very much like me
    g. Mostly like me
    h. Somewhat like me
    i. Not much like me
    j. Not like me at all
11. I become interested in new pursuits every few months.*
    k. Very much like me
    l. Mostly like me
    m. Somewhat like me
    n. Not much like me
    o. Not like me at all
12. I am diligent.
    p. Very much like me
    q. Mostly like me
    r. Somewhat like me
    s. Not much like me
    t. Not like me at all

Scoring:

1. For questions 1, 4, 6, 9, 10, and 12, assign the following points:

5 = Very much like me
4 = Mostly like me
3 = Somewhat like me
2 = Not much like me
1 = Not like me at all

2. For questions 2, 3, 5, 7, 8, and 11, assign the following points:

1 = Very much like me
2 = Mostly like me
3 = Somewhat like me
4 = Not much like me
5 = Not like me at all

Add up all the points and divide by 12. The maximum score on this scale is 5 (extremely gritty), and the lowest score on this scale is 1 (not at all gritty).

What is your grit score? Reflect a little on the score you have and write what comes to you.

_____
_____
_____
_____
_____
_____
_____
_____
_____

Duckworth, A.L., Peterson, C., Matthews, M.D., and Kelly, D.R. (2007). Grit: Perseverance and Passion for Long-Term Goals. *Journal of Personality and Social Psychology*. Vol. 92. 1087–1101.[4]

"People don't buy WHAT you do, they buy WHY you do it."

—Simon Sinek

Creating Your "Why" Statement (also known as your Impact Statement)

Your legacy becomes your "why." Your "why" drives you from the moment you find it until the moment you leave this earth. Your "why" may slightly change over the years, but more often, it does not. You end up acquiring other "whys" along the way due to your own life metamorphosis. But for right now, I want you to take a few moments to think about your "why." Your "why" is also known as your impact statement. What impact do you desire to have in this world? Your "why" can never be money. It must be something deeper than that. Your "why," along with your divine talents and abilities, will steer you in life and keep you on course. Everyone needs a "why." I am going to share one of mine with you, and then I want you to think about yours. I have provided space for you to write it out.

"My 'why' is deeply rooted in my desire to help others heal and be free from the trauma they have gone through in their lives. One out of every four girls is abused, and one out of every five boys is abused. I was abused from ages 3–13, then at ages 13–16 I went through another form of abuse. At age 16, I was a freshman in high school and living on my own. This is only a portion of the abuse I endured. One of the greatest callings in my life is to be used to help heal others. I will not only write a book, but I will write multiple books. I will also be speaking on a national and international level. I have many gifts that I plan to use fully. I have learned over time that I have been honored to have to endure what I have and still make it out. Now I give back!"

Now it is your turn. Give it a try. If you need time to think about it, then do that—think. Go to your core. Find your purpose within, and then write out your "why." After you find it, put it up where you can see it. Let it lead you in the direction that you truly desire to go.

Goal Setting

You should always be setting goals. When you set your goals, you will need to think about what steps to take in order to accomplish them. I will ask you to set goals several times in this workbook. For this section, the goals I want you to reflect on will be your life goals. What are the things you what for your life? I want you to really think and don't hold back. Nothing is impossible. With the right mindset, you can achieve what you set out to achieve. I am living proof of that. Once you understand what you really want for your life, then you will be able to start working on the steps you need to take to accomplish those dreams and life goals. I encourage you as you sit with this activity to take several deep breaths and allow yourself to be in a calm state. You may even wish to meditate and actually see your "self" in the future. There is a future you calling you to your higher self. Think about that. Let that give you encouragement. You may even write yourself a goal letter. Write the letter to yourself, say, in ten years or even twenty years. What do you want to accomplish? What dreams do you wish to see manifested by then? What level of education will you have acquired by then? The questions are endless. Give it a try. Make sure to sign it and date it. Then in the future, you can read what you wrote and see how well you did.

Creating a Vision Board

Did you know that caterpillars have something called "imaginal cells"? They are cells that are, well, imagined. You see, once the caterpillar has eaten enough food, the new imaginal cells come forward. A new way of thinking begins. This becomes even more apparent after the struggle in the cocoon—the struggle for the caterpillar to morph into the beautiful butterfly it was purposed to be. The caterpillar and the butterfly both have a purpose, as each of us does. No matter what stage we are at in our lives, understanding our purpose is critical to being empowered.

Vision, just like purpose, is also critical to our journey. You may be surprised at how many major deals close on one fact: the investor can see that the startup founder is a visionary. When you are a visionary, you bring the extraordinary to life. Your mindset is creative and not limited. Thought that is no longer limited will result in experiences that are no longer limited. The visionary knows this because their thoughts are not limited.

Visionaries are able to manifest things. Vision boards are a great way to activate your vision. I have several vision boards. I have seen many things come to fruition through my boards. When I create them, I not only think about the vision, but I have learned how to feel the vision bringing the heart and the mind together. If you are hoping for rain in the desert, you must not just pray for it. You must feel the rain. You must smell the rain. You must be wearing rain gear and be prepared for the rain. This is the heart of vision—the feeling of it. If you truly want to go from startup to success, then you need to not only see yourself and your business succeeding, you need to feel it. You need to feel what it is like to wear imported silk suits. You need to feel what it is like to sit at the top of your high-rise office building. The feeling is the part that brings it to life.

Empowered entrepreneurs do not predict the future; they create it. Your final task will be to create a vision board. There are several ways you can create your vision board. You can gather magazines and cut out pictures or words. You will need glue sticks and poster board to place the pictures on.

You can also use a computer and google different things that represent your vision and then save the pictures. You can take those pictures and place them in a Word document. You could even create it in Adobe Photoshop. You could use your smartphone (same concept as with a computer). Google the things you desire for yourself, your business, your life, your family, and so on. Then save the pictures to your camera roll. You will need a collage maker—there are many free apps out there that can make picture collages. Then place whichever pictures you like in the collage. TA-DA! You now have your vision board.

While creating the vision board, you really want to be connected in thought and heart. See yourself in the boat that you just cut out. Feel the breeze as you walk the beach and watch the sunset in the picture of Bali that is now on your board. See the increase in financial freedom and see that you are rich in love, time, talents, and the like. I use a lot of words in my vision boards, as words are my love language. What is your love language? If it is words, then make sure to use lots of positive words on your board.

The vision board needs to be placed where you can see it every day. For the one you did with your phone, you may save it as your lock screen or background. You could even send it to be printed as a photograph. For your Word document boards, you can print them out in color, but black and white will do, too. The poster board method is simple: just put that sucker up on your wall. Put them all up on your wall. Look at them. Let them breathe and live within you. Go back to feeling your vision and believing in it. Before you know it, you will be driving the Camaro you put on your board. You will be floating in a hot air balloon ride. You will be walking the streets of Rome. All of what I just listed, from the Camaro to Rome, were on my vision board and have come to reality. I could go on and on, but now I want you to give it a try.

Please remember this one thing: the vision is for an appointed time. Though it may tarry, it will not be late. For everything there is a season. You must be patient and know that your vision will come to pass if you faint not.

Remember the caterpillar and the imaginal cells I told you about at the beginning of this section? We, too, have such cells. They come forward as we transform our lives. Your vision is your imaginal cells. It is your higher purpose. I am sure the caterpillar had its doubts, and I can only imagine its friends and family gave it a hard time. *You're back imagining things, aren't you? You really believe you have a higher purpose? You are so low to the ground that the only thing that has you beat is a snake. Come on now. You think you will really fly one day?* Have you ever been mocked by your friends or family for what you imagined? What you believed your higher power to be? I have, and it hurt. But with the same confidence of a caterpillar that walked so low to the ground, I believed that I had imaginal cells—my higher purpose cells. And at the right time, in the right season, I would go into a very dark place. I would let go of my family, friends, and foes. I would transform, and then I would struggle just a little more. Finally, I would break through the cocoon—the most beautiful imagined butterfly you ever saw in your life.

Now, go create your imaginal cells. It is time for you to grow. Healthy things grow. Growing things change. Change is good. You have the power in your mind to be whatever you desire. But faith is dead without work. And so is vision. You must execute. The remaining chapters will provide you with the knowledge and the tools you need to help increase your ability to execute. Before you know it, you will be flying in the air with me. Welcome to *Startup to Success!*

Create Your Vision Board Here

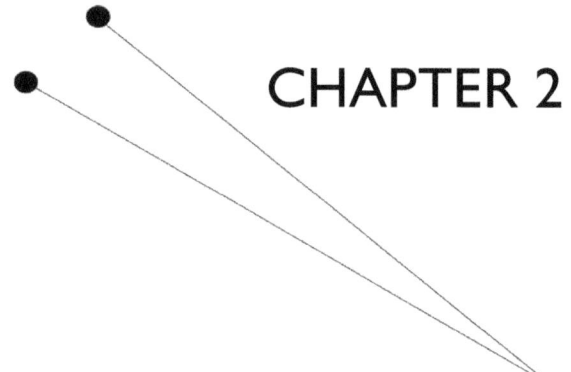

CHAPTER 2

Time and Project Management

"The common man is not concerned about the passage of time; the man of talent is driven by it."

—Arthur Schopenhauer

You are extraordinary, and you have talents. Did you know that? Well, you do! Therefore, you will need to be driven by time. But you will not let time drive you. You can learn to master it. And master it you must in order to go from startup to success. I want you to read over the following information, which comes from Doreen Virtue's best-selling book, *Don't Let Anything Dull Your Sparkle: How to Break Free of Negativity and Drama.*

"One source of stress is the way in which you view and manage time. How often have you been upset because you're running late or behind on a deadline? Time pressure is a major source of stress. Chronic lateness can also lead to relationship arguments. Your brain under stress is focused on surviving and reacting, and less focused upon planning and creating. With chronic stress, your brain learns—and is rewired—to be focused upon survival and *reacting only. It has difficulty amping up the area devoted to devising plans for the future. Constant time urgency takes a toll on your body, brain, and emotions. Here are some time-urgency patterns and ways to heal them:*

Approval seeking: *A mindset of I must get everything done right now, or I will be in trouble or something bad will happen comes from the desire to prove yourself or to appease a real or imaginary authority figure. Usually, this stems from a childhood where you were working overtime to gain parental acceptance. As an adult, you can transfer the desire to win outside approval to a healthy desire to give yourself approval. And that comes from taking positive action steps, such as peacefully working instead of frantically racing against the clock.*

Forcing yourself: *If you find yourself starting a sentence with the words "I have to..." stop and question why you're doing what you're doing. Why are you forcing and pushing yourself? That's a sign that your soul is rejecting the activity and it isn't healthy. Either meditate and get to the point where you are happy to engage in the activity, make changes with respect to how you engage in it (switching to a more enjoyable workout routine, for example), or stop doing it altogether.*

Indecisiveness: *The thought I can't decide whether to do this or do that can make you feel stuck. The existential dilemma of having to make choices concerning how to spend time is the basis of internal struggles and angst. Remember that not making a decision is the same thing as making one...because if you aren't making a decision, you're deciding to stay in your present state. Sometimes life calls you to make a choice before you're ready. Do your best and go for what your soul calls you to do.*

Not planning ahead: *Part of drama addition is procrastinating until an appointment or deadline is upon you. Do you wait until Christmas Eve to shop for gifts, or the night before a report is due to begin it? These are examples of needlessly stressing yourself. Planning ahead is a new habit that can substantially lower your stress levels. One way to plan is to break a big task down into small steps, and then schedule them into your calendar.*

Stressing to impress: Are you working like crazy to make enough money to buy prestigious items? Who are you trying to impress? This unhealthy and stressful habit stems from a desire to be loved. However, if people like you for what you own, it's a hallow feeling. You desire and deserve to be loved for who you are…beginning with loving yourself for having a calmer, more peaceful schedule.

Being a martyr: Do you feel resentful and irritable because you have to do all of the work? This is stressful and toxic, and a sign that you need to (a) look for ways to simplify your life so that you're not bemoaning how much you have to do, and or (b) start delegating tasks and asking others to help you.

Focusing upon the future: After a trauma, it's natural to worry whether something painful will recur. However, if you become obsessed with fear about possible future traumas, you'll lose the enjoyment of the moment. This is a part of post-traumatic dissociations, where you lose present awareness of yourself. A simple and effective method for reconnecting with the present is to de deep breathing. Inhale deeply, and then exhale completely. Notice your heart rate. Be aware of whether you're comfortable or not. What do you see and hear right now? Focusing upon present feelings and environmental cues help center you in the here and now. This empowers you to feel more confident about your present and your future."[5]

Now that you have read the content above, I want you spend some time reflecting and make note of what stood out to you from what you read. Where do you see yourself? How can you change for the better?

Reflection:
_____
_____
_____
_____
_____

To multitask or to not? That is the question. Do you know that multitasking is an illusion? As an empowered entrepreneur, you must be focused. You must stop multitasking. It only trains the brain to be distracted. Instead, focus on one small task at a time. Treat your mind like a muscle. It takes time to build up muscle by going to the gym, lifting weights, and eating right. The same is true with the mind. Any weightlifter will tell you that you don't lift your arm weights and press your legs at the same time. You do one exercise at a time. You do that one with pure focus, deliberate practice, and you build by repetition.

Do not become addicted to the rush of constantly being busy. For some individuals, there is confusion between being "on the go" and actually accomplishing what one needs to accomplish. Many of these people view themselves as successful multitaskers. This ability to multitask is often referred to as a modern-day requisite skill. However, the reality is that multitasking appears to reduce one's productivity. Some studies indicate that multitasking prolongs the accomplishment of a list of tasks by as much as 20–40 percent.[6]

To learn even more about how you manage and handle time, I want you to track your time. Tracking is a tool used in business many times over. The more you can track, the more you can learn. You can see what is working and what is not. Most importantly, you can make changes for the better and become more efficient. On the next page, you will find your tracking challenge. You will track your time for one week. You will write what day of the week it is and what the date is. Then you will write your start and stop times and indicate what you were doing during those times. You need to be honest. This challenge is to help you grow. You can reflect daily on the time you have tracked, or you can reflect at the end once you have tracked your time for a full week. The goal is to see how you are spending your time and then make the necessary adjustments so you can use your time better. There will be space for you to write your reflection at the end of the tracking sheets. This challenge will be very eye-opening if you are true to it. Remember, this is to help you grow.

Track Your Time Challenge

Date	Day of the week	Start Time	Stop Time	Task/Activity (what did you do during this time)

Date	Day of the week	Start Time	Stop Time	Task/Activity (what did you do during this time)

Reflection:

"Good fortune is what happens when opportunity meets with planning."

—Thomas Edison

Let's now turn our attention to project management. You must have some basic understanding of project management in order to go from startup to success. Projects, by nature, are unique and will vary. What's important is to understand how to break down projects into what are called milestones. I am a project manager by nature. As a professor, I give my students their final project broken down into milestones. This takes a large project and makes it more doable to the mind. Projects are also temporary, and they are fluid. They will have a start and a stop to them. According to the book *Project Management* by Adrienne Watt, there are four phases to any project. They are as follows:

1. Initiation Phase
2. Planning Phase
3. Implementation (Execution) Phase
4. Closing Phase

"*Initiation Phase*

During the first of these phases, the initiation phase, the project objective or need is identified; this can be a business problem or opportunity. An appropriate response to the need is documented in a business case with recommended solution options. A feasibility study is conducted to investigate whether each option addresses the project objective and a final recommended solution is determined. Issues of feasibility ("can we do the project?") and justification ("should we do the project?") are addressed.

Once the recommended solution is approved, a project is initiated to deliver the approved solution and a project manager is appointed. The major deliverables and the participating work groups are identified, and the project team begins to take shape. Approval is then sought by the project manager to move onto the detailed planning phase.

Planning Phase

The next phase, the planning phase, is where the project solution is further developed in as much detail as possible and the steps necessary to meet the project's objective are planned. In this step, the team identifies all of the work to be done. The project's tasks and resource requirements are identified, along with the strategy for producing them. This is also referred to as "scope management." A project plan is created outlining the activities, tasks, dependencies, and timeframes. The project manager coordinates the preparation of a project budget by providing cost estimates for the labor, equipment, and materials costs. The budget is used to monitor and control cost expenditures during project implementation.

Once the project team has identified the work, prepared the schedule, and estimated the costs, the three fundamental components of the planning process are complete. This is an excellent time to identify and try to deal with anything that might pose a threat to the successful completion of the project. This is called risk management. In risk management, "high-threat" potential problems are identified along with the action that is to be taken on each high-threat potential problem, either to reduce the probability that the problem will occur or to reduce the impact on the project if it does occur. This is also a good time to identify all project stakeholders and establish a communication plan describing the information needed and the delivery method to be used to keep the stakeholders informed.

Finally, you will want to document a quality plan, providing quality targets, assurance, and control measures, along with an acceptance plan, listing the criteria to be met to gain customer acceptance. At this point, the project would have been planned in detail and is ready to be executed.

Implementation (Execution) Phase

During the third phase, the implementation phase, the project plan is put into motion and the work of the project is performed. It is important to *maintain control and communicate as needed during implementation. Progress is continuously monitored and appropriate adjustments are made and recorded as variances from the original plan. In any project, a project manager spends most of the time in this step. During project implementation, people are carrying out the tasks, and progress information is being reported through regular team meetings. The project manager uses this information to maintain control over the direction of the project by comparing the progress reports with the project plan to measure the performance of the project activities and take corrective action as needed. The first course of action should always be to bring the project back on course (i.e., to return it to the original plan). If that cannot happen, the team should record variations from the original plan and record and publish modifications to the plan. Throughout this step, project sponsors and other key stakeholders should be kept informed of the project's status according to the agreed-on frequency and format of communication. The plan should be updated and published on a regular basis.*

Status reports should always emphasize the anticipated end point in terms of cost, schedule, and quality of deliverables. Each project deliverable produced should be reviewed for quality and measured against the acceptance criteria. Once all of the deliverables have been produced and the customer has accepted the final solution, the project is ready for closure.

Closing Phase

During the final closure, or completion phase, the emphasis is on releasing the final deliverables to the customer, handing over project documentation to the business, terminating supplier contracts, releasing project resources, and communicating the closure of the project to all stakeholders. The last remaining step is to conduct lessons-learned studies to examine what went well and what didn't. Through this type of analysis, the wisdom of experience is transferred back to the project organization, which will help future project teams."[7]

Now let's break down what you just read into a more digestible model. Initiation: before you start any project large or small, you will need to define your goals. You will take those goals and create actionable steps. This your planning stage. You will set your milestones in this phase and you will identify the key partners, resources, and the like. All of which you will need to help you accomplish the task at hand. You will then move into the implementation (execution) phase. This is where the rubber meets the road, as the saying goes. You better be ready to work in order to see that this project actually moves from milestone to milestone. Then, it is a wrap (closing phase). You will have seen the project to completion, and you will then reflect on how it all went. You will need to make sure to track all that took place from the start of the project to the finish. You will use this information to help you make adjustments as needed for future projects. You will also know who your strong players are, and who is a liability. You will need to make sure to cut all liabilities.

Here are some additional tips according to a recent blog by Project Manager:

"Be Specific

You need to spend a bit of time and energy thinking through what you want to achieve and what impact you want to have. It isn't enough to say something like, "We want to grow our business." To give projects a sense of purpose and focus, you'd need to take this general idea and sharpen it. You'd say something like, "We want to grow our business by 10% this quarter by creating a new service line for our existing customers." This is a pretty simple example, but it drills down from a vague idea to a specific set of goals. This applies to any type of business, because all projects need to have focus, regardless of the industry.

Stay Flexible

As an entrepreneur or startup, you must be comfortable with change. Change happens, and when you're blazing a new trail, being able to pivot is key to success. Whatever plan you create today is only a starting point for where you are going to go in the future. But you still need to have a plan that starts with the end in mind. Where are you going? When do you need to get there? What kind of resources do you have or need? What other factors are involved in getting this project completed?

Don't Waste Resources

An inefficient organization (and startups can't afford to be inefficient) can spend a lot of time expending resources on things that never should have received valuable resources in the first place. That's probably the number-one takeaway from project management: do the due diligence of asking yourself the where, what, why, when and how before beginning any project.

Know When to Fold 'em

One roadblock that startups and entrepreneurs encounter is the unwillingness to recognize and accept sunk costs. By this I mean, if your goal or outcome isn't relevant anymore, but you're so far into the project that you won't let go. You think it might have a negative impact on the team. The best thing to do is to quit things that need to be abandoned. Knowing when to quit is a bit of an art. If you struggle with it, read Seth Godin's book The Dip. He writes about knowing when to quit and when to stay the course.

Lessons Learned for Future Projects

Creating a resource that helps you accelerate the kickoff of future projects is the key to ending a project well. Depending on your nature and your organization, these documents collected may be complex, or they may be loose. Again, the important thing is to make sure you have collected things to look for and things to avoid so that you don't have to relearn everything every time you start a project."[8]

Here are some steps to take in order to create a project plan:

1. *"Create Task Lists: Create a task list that details steps for every task throughout the project. Then, prioritize this list to effectively assign team members and resources. Tasks vary in how essential they are to*

the project. As you prioritize tasks, it's likely you'll find some tasks that can be sacrificed completely to increase efficiency.

2. *Establish Duration: Once tasks have been compiled and prioritized, the next step is to establish how long they will take. Duration of tasks, here, will likely be an educated guess. No matter, it's important to use all the tools you have available—including past experiences—to make the best possible estimation.*

3. *Outline Dependencies: Not all tasks are the same. Some are dependent tasks. A dependent task is a task that can't be started until another task has been completed. When crafting your project plan, it's important to identify these dependent tasks from the outset. Dependent tasks can derail a project plan if too many team members are waiting for completion. It's vital to note dependent tasks on your project plan so they can be linked. This linking shows team members the importance of one task being completed before another can be started.*

4. *Develop a Resource Plan: Completing tasks on time requires the development of a resource plan. This is the final transitional step between project phases. Resources, in this context, include everything from team members, to office equipment, to the software you'll use to plan and execute your project. It's important to identify all resources so they can be managed effectively."*[9]

As you learn to become a master of both your time and your projects, you will be a force to be reckoned with. You will find that there is nothing you cannot accomplish if you put your mind to it and use the talents of time control and project management to your advantage. Then you will go from startup to success in no time at all.

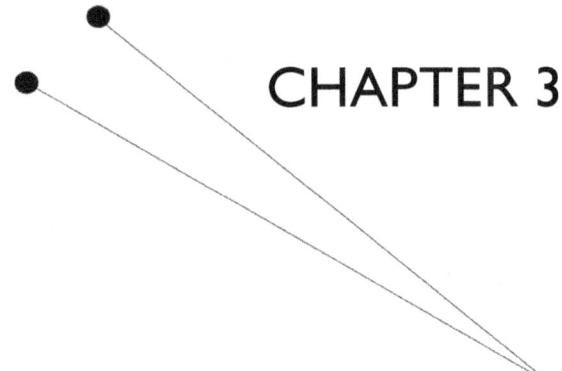

CHAPTER 3

Human-Centered Design Thinking

"Whatever the mind can conceive and believe, the mind can achieve."

—Napoleon Hill, *Think and Grow Rich*

Before we jump into human-centered design thinking, I want us to take a look at the common thread that connects all empowered entrepreneurs. Do you know what it is? The mind. Remember me stating this in Chapter 1? There are two types of mindsets: fixed and growth. The fixed mindset is very constraining and keeps us bound. The growth mindset, on the other hand, is very liberating. The fixed mindset believes that talent and intelligence are all that's needed to be successful. The fixed mindset does not take well to criticism or failure, and normally only sees one way. The growth mindset believes that talent and intelligence, combined with hard work, will win every time. Even in failure, the growth mindset sees a winning score. The growth mindset is a lifelong learner and never turns down an opportunity to better oneself. The growth mindset understands the importance of practice and being dedicated to pursuing goals. The growth mindset goes through setbacks with an innate ability to persevere. The growth mindset is gritty.

The empowered entrepreneur has a growth mindset—also known as the entrepreneurial mindset. The entrepreneurial mindset sees opportunity where others see obstacles. It sees solutions where others only see fires. The entrepreneurial mindset has vision, and no vision is too radical, too far-fetched, or too insane. It believes that anything is possible—that no matter how long it takes, every dream will come to pass. The life desired is going to be lived. Nothing stops the entrepreneurial mindset. It is *EMPOWERED!*

How we see ourselves is directly related to how we will lead our lives. If you believe that your talents are fixed or set in stone, then you will stay stuck. You will keep repeating one hell of a rollercoaster ride by trying to prove yourself over and over again. You will stay in the valley of validation when you simply need to walk in the victory of being your authentic self. Stop wasting time trying to prove how great you are—try to grow and get better. When I work with business owners, I want to see them go from good to great, from great to amazing, and even then, I encourage them to keep growing. I want to see them struggle and go through growing pains. I encourage them to stretch themselves, to go to the ultra-limits of their lives. That is where they become ridiculously amazing. That is how you go from startup to success.

"Float like a butterfly. Sting like a bee."

—Muhammad Ali, World Champion boxer

Muhammad Ali was one of the greatest boxers of all time. His success is directly related to his ability to think systematically, which created thought patterns and processes that attracted greatness to him. He was a very skilled and talented boxer and would out-practice anyone. As an empowered entrepreneur, you need to be skilled like Ali. You need to have his same work ethic. You need to understand the power of your unique frequency, which is your thought process. You need to settle for nothing less than greatness. You will need to understand your unique talents. There are four talents that are critical to being an empowered entrepreneur:

- Imagination
- Experimentation
- Insight
- Wisdom

When was the last time you played? I mean freely played, when your imagination just ran wild. Do you remember being a child and playing without a care in the world? There are so many benefits to playing—most importantly, the ability to heighten our imagination. When we can imagine with no self-censorship getting in the way, no pressure from the matrix telling us we are getting it wrong, we become liberated. So much learning can be found no matter what form of play you encounter. Imagination is sparked. As an empowered entrepreneur, it is important that you develop the talent of imagination. It opens the mind, and when the mind is open, there is no limit to what it can and will produce. Imagination also activates creativity.

I'm always surprised at the number of people who believe they are not creative. Now, I understand that some people are not that crafty. I get that part, but when mothers especially tell me they are not that creative, I think to myself, *How is that? You created a human, for God's sake!* Imagination and creativity open a whole new level of thinking for you. It is that key that finds solutions to problems. But do you know what blocks creativity? FEAR. Yes, fear. **F**alse **E**vidence **A**ppearing **R**eal. Fear is an emotional roadblock. Before we even get started being creative, fear pops in with self-doubt and insecurity. Then we self-censor. The mind is so powerful, but when limited, it is very weak. You must turn the self-censor off and stop dancing with your complex issue. Pick up the brush of creativity and paint your future. The empowered entrepreneur doesn't predict his or her future; they imagine it. They create it.

The talent of experimentation is why scientists are so damn cool. Without experimentation, we would not have many of the inventions we have today, nor would we have the future. Thomas Edison is one of my favorite inventors of all time. Do you know how many times he failed while creating the light bulb? So many times! But it was through experimentation that he finally arrived at the light bulb, and that sucker is everywhere today. Get out of the building or office and go experiment. Go try your product on the consumer. Go test your theory in the marketplace. Then you will know which next steps to take with your services or products. Everything in entrepreneurship is about action and trying. When you experiment, you become open to learning about how new processes would work for your organization and ways to effectively cut costs in order to help manage cash flow. Again, there is no limit to what experimenting can do for you as you launch, manage, and grow your business.

One of the best places for you to do some experimenting is at a makerspace. A makerspace is a collaborative workspace. Co-working spaces can also be rented for startup businesses. You will find all kinds of elements at a makerspace—from 3D printers to sewing machines. Everything from coding to the creation of art takes place in a makerspace. It is a hub for genius and creativity. You can use most of the equipment found there. You will need to learn how to use the equipment first, of course, but after that, you are good to go. If you are in my class at one of the colleges or in my virtual course, you will be introduced to our makerspace. There are makerspaces everywhere—all you have do is search online for them, and I am sure you will find one in your area. I encourage you to go explore and experiment.

Another skill that's critical to life and business is insight. The definition of insight is "*the capacity to gain an accurate and deep intuitive understanding of a person or thing.*" In essence, insight is being empathic. A study at the University of Michigan revealed that empathy levels in our world have dropped dramatically—"*College kids today are about 40 percent lower in empathy than their counterparts of 20 or 30 years ago.*"[10] I am so shocked at how much we just don't care for humankind. Being able to relate and understand your clients' needs or your customers' needs is the golden key to maintaining their loyalty and business. Being able to put yourself in someone else's shoes will open your mind, enabling you to create better solutions for them. You may create products or services that fit their needs which were unmet prior to your solutions. This is only one of the reasons why insight is so important to have, not only as an empowered entrepreneur, but as a human being.

Some people, who are what we call "empaths," believe they are cursed. But I am here to set the record straight: you are far from cursed. You are gifted, and we need your gift more today than ever before.

Wisdom is timeless. Many people are wise with age, and some never carry wisdom at all because they do not take time to reflect. As an empowered entrepreneur, I demand action. I am results-driven. But I never negate the power of reflection, and in business, you must have both action and reflection in equal measure. It is in the reflection that we gain wisdom. How often do you reflect? When doing so, it is important to have a pen and notepad available, or your computer if you'd like. Write it all out, from the good to the bad to the ugly. Even reflecting on the weather or season is critical. Take note of the time of day and your energy level—all very important pieces to your puzzle. To be successful in any area, you must exercise wisdom and plan carefully. If wisdom is to bring you prosperity, joy, admiration, and longevity, then you must be disciplined and reflect daily.

Do you have what it takes to go from startup to success? It all starts in the mind. You must have a mind that is up to the challenge. You must have the talents mentioned above operating in your life on a daily basis. You must go to your core and walk in your authentic self. You must get in the dirt and never be afraid of hard work. Life is short, even on the longest day. I need you to roll with the punches, and when the opportunity presents itself, go for it.

> "Human-centered design is a philosophy, not a precise set of methods, but one that assumes that innovation should start by getting close to users and observing their activities."
>
> —Donald A. Norman, co-founder of Nielsen Norman Group

All of the talents we just covered play a role in human-centered design thinking. The process is all about how to take on problem-solving in a creative way, geared with the human in mind. We are, after all, looking to solve problems and get the job done. According to IDEO's website, *"Human-centered design is about cultivating deep empathy with the people you're designing for; generating ideas; building a bunch of prototypes; sharing what you've made with the people you're designing for; and eventually, putting your innovative new solution out in the world."*[11]

According to the nonprofit organization Ideo.org, human-centered design consists of three steps:

1. *"**Inspiration**: Identify the problem. Interview people impacted by the problem. Employ empathy and active listening to fully understand how the end-user/customer is impacted. What are other factors that may play a role?*
2. ***Ideation**: After gathering information and interviewing, brainstorm ideas on how to solve the problem. Think of all factors, including end-users, constraints such as budget, and be creative. Develop prototypes to test out.*
3. ***Implementation**: Implement the idea and document how it is being used. Accept and apply feedback. Iterate on the original concept to make it even stronger."*[12]

According to DC Design, human-centered design thinking is broken down into five phases:

1. "***Empathize***

The foundational principle of human-centered design is that you should truly understand the people who experience a problem before you design a solution to serve them. Empathy is about understanding the problem by immersing yourself in the community that will be affected by your design. Designers spend time talking directly with those who experience a problem, observing how their environments work, and consulting experts on the issue to fully grasp all the challenges that need to be overcome in order to create a solution. This stage, and the design process as a whole, is about asking questions instead of making assumptions about why things are the way they are. Those who can adopt a "learner's mindset" when approaching problems that affect other people will have the greatest success in creating solutions that make an impact.

This is the most important part of the process, focusing on participatory action research—not just documenting the user, but engaging them in the brainstorming, modeling, and prototyping as well.

2. **Define**

This step helps set up the rest of the process. After learning as much as you can about the issue you're looking to solve, define the problem by focusing on the key action that you want to accomplish. Most often people try to define problems as a mix of problem and solution. Some examples of the statements we've heard are "We need more money." "We need to pass a law." "We need to build more jails."

These statements are bad examples of how to define a problem. As a human centered designer, you should always be asking why. Why do we need more jails? What are we really trying to accomplish? The answer might be something like, "We need a way to maintain public safety." That's the real problem you want to focus on. The way you define the problem is important and should be phrased in a way that allows for creativity in how it could be addressed.

With this statement, designers can come up with a variety of potential solutions. This statement will serve as the thesis that the team can repeatedly check solutions against throughout the process to ensure that they're actually tackling all aspects of the problem.

3. Ideate

Now having come to better understand the perspective of the person who experiences the problem during the empathy phase and defining an actionable problem in the define stage, it's brainstorm time. Come up with as many solutions to the problem you defined as possible. This is best done in teams where each team member writes down the ideas they have one at a time and place them on a board for everyone to see. One key thing to keep in mind here is that this isn't the time to judge whether ideas are good or bad, practical or outlandish. The goal is to come up with as many ideas as possible. When we judge ideas as they come out, it shuts down the creative process. Often an impractical idea scaled back slightly can become exactly the type of novel solution that you're looking for.

Additionally, don't be afraid to include those who live with a problem in the brainstorming process. At DC Design we embrace a concept known as co-design where we work right alongside those we are aiming to design for. By having them involved in the process, you're likely to get more nuanced solutions that are bottom-up, not top-down.

4. Prototype

Designers put ideas to action by creating low-cost experiments to test their ideas. These experiments or prototypes can be created for physical products, virtual interfaces, processes, or systems. In any of these situations, the goal is to create something you can test with those who live with the problem in order to see if it works. For physical and virtual products, this is often a model of the designs you have in mind. In the case of services, build out a model with actionable steps and a workflow that can be simulate either in the real world or through role-play. Given that it's a prototype, it's considered a work in progress, not a final solution. A good practice is for designers and participants to have multiple prototypes and experiment to see which one is best suited to meet the needs of the person they are designing for.

5. Test and Iterate

Put the ideas and prototypes to test. This is where designers identify flaws, weaknesses, and gaps in the design, improving it along the way. The person who lives with the problem is asked to test the model or the prototype repeatedly and see if it addresses all aspects of a problem. It is particularly important when testing that you are not trying to defend your solution. Your goal is to use your prototype as a way of learning more about the people you are designing for. What do they like about it? What don't they like about it? Why is that? If you can look at this as an opportunity to learn more about what the best solution would look like for those who need it, you'll be able to produce a solution that has significantly more uptake than one where you forced your ideas through.

While this may seem like the end, the design process is meant to be dynamic and cyclical. It is often not linear, but you will only realize what your next step is once you are in the midst of the design process. For instance, in the prototyping stage, one might realize that the ideas they are prototyping don't actually meet the need that was defined. That might mean the designer needs to brainstorm further or understand nuances of the problem even more deeply. So that would take them back to earlier stages in the process. This is a fluid, continuous process until all the participants are satisfied and a solution has been identified that truly addresses the problem. Stick with it! The cycles get shorter the further along you go and the more you practice using it."[13]

Now I want you to give it a try. How can you use this model to help you problem solve with creativity for your clients and customers? Take some time to reflect and write what comes to mind with regards to each phase we have covered.

Reflection:

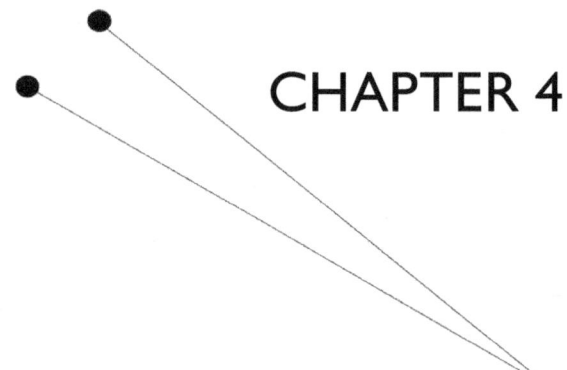

CHAPTER 4

Business Legal Structure and Intellectual Property

"Mistakes are the growing pains of wisdom."

—William George Jordan, writer and editor

One of the most common mistakes I see in early stages of entrepreneurship is how a startup legally forms its business. This is not an area to take lightly. You will need to carefully consider all options and what each one means to you now and in the future. I will give you fair warning: I am not for one particular legal structure over the other. Just like a project is unique, so is each business. I've been a sole proprietor for all eighteen years that I've been in business. I'm fully protected with insurance, too. I do have a DBA, also known as "Doing Business As," but sole proprietorship is the most common way to form a business. However, it is not the only way to form your business. Let's take a deeper dive into what some of your options are.

Business Legal Structures

I have so many stories from students and clients who tell me how they structured their business as a limited liability company (LLC) and only ended up with a large tax bill. They didn't even generate any profit from their business. What they failed to do was really take time to ask themselves some important questions.

The first step in structuring your business is to assess your risks. What are they? Could insurance cover low risk? What type of investments do you have that someone could take? Do you need to be an LLC or corporation to get a contract or do a particular type of work? Do you really need to be an LLC or corporation? I need you to think carefully about these questions. The answers will determine how you structure your business. It is critical that you do as much research as possible. Don't make the mistake of choosing the wrong structure. When choosing your business structure, it is wise to consult with a business lawyer or even a tax accountant. Both will help you make a sound decision.

Sole proprietorship is the simplest, most inexpensive, and most common business structure. Sole means one owner. Because the man who previously owned my business was a sole proprietor, I naturally became one as well. As a sole proprietor, I have no protection. The liability is all mine. That is the most important takeaway for sole proprietorship: you are not protected. Of course, there is insurance to acquire, and we will discuss the different types of insurance a little later in the book.

According to the SBA, "*sole proprietorships do not produce a separate business entity. This means your business assets and liabilities are not separate from your personal assets and liabilities. You can be held personally liable for the debts and obligations of the business.*"[14] Just because you begin as a sole proprietor doesn't mean you will stay one. Amazon is a perfect example of a company that started as a sole proprietorship, and now Amazon is clearly ruling the world! Okay, so it's not ruling the world, but it is now a publicly traded corporation.

Sole proprietorship is extremely easy to form. In many areas, there is no legal filing fee at all to be a sole proprietor. If you choose to use a business name, you will need to research your local county's process to file for a DBA, also known as **D**oing **B**usiness **A**s. Your DBA becomes your legal name and you are then able to open a business bank account. My DBA is Start To Finish Files. Having a DBA adds to your professionalism. This doesn't mean you cannot use your name—many people do. The decision is up to you and what works best for your business. Your business may fall in an area or industry that requires licenses or permits. In that case, you will have a small fee to pay and you will need to make sure to keep up with the renewal of those licenses and permits so you don't incur additional charges.

Taxes for a sole proprietorship are simple as well. They are seen as personal taxes. Remember, you and your business are one entity, which means you are together. You will file one tax return, which will lay out your expenses and your income. There is a self-employment tax that you need to be aware of—it is fairly large, and when you first encounter it, it may shock you. You will want to visit the Internal Revenue Service's website and explore the detailed information regarding taxation for sole proprietorship. After all, they are the ones you are paying the money to.

"The best partnerships aren't dependent on a mere common goal but on a shared path of equality, desire, and no small amount of passion."

—Sarah MacLean, author

Partnerships are another way many businesses are structured. Partnerships are two or more people who share in the building of a business. Partnerships are an interesting dance, like the two-step; however, not everyone can do the two-step, nor should they try. Understanding yourself is key to knowing whether or not a partnership will work for you. I am a controller, so most partnerships do not work for me. I need to be in control and call the shots. I am very comfortable raising people up to lead, as that is part of the business I am in. However, I need them to go lead on another ship, not mine. They come to me to be trained, and I send them out to lead and train others.

Setting up a partnership is simple to do. You don't even need a contract, but I highly recommend that you do have a contract to protect yourself. It must be detailed, and it must hold all relevant information, such as who will be doing what (roles), who will make decisions, who will handle the money, who gets what cut of the money, who will hold the most liability, and how will the business dissolve. There are many templates out there regarding partnership contracts. My advice is to research them and find one that works best for you and your partner(s). You can always edit a template to make it yours. You should also consider taking the document to a lawyer for review—or even have them create one for you. What you don't want to do is go into business with someone regardless of how much you trust or love them, without a written contract in hand.

Have you ever heard of a "silent partner"? Silent partners are found in **limited partnerships** (LP). According to the SBA, "*Limited partnerships have only one general partner with unlimited liability, and all other partners have limited liability. The partners with limited liability also tend to have limited control over the company, which is documented in a partnership agreement. Profits are passed through to personal tax returns, and the general partner—the partner without limited liability—must also pay self-employment taxes.*"[14]

One example of an LP is a gym. Many times, there are multiple owners in a gym. I was a member of a local gym that was set up as an LP. The staff and members actually loved the silent partner. He would come in from time to time and work on things in the gym, but the general manager was a real jerk. He needed to get off the juice, in my opinion. The general manager made some poor business decisions, but the limited partner, though he didn't agree with the decisions, was not able to change them. He had to remain silent. The problem with an LP is that someone else, just like the gym case given, can make poor business decisions, which ultimately will have a direct effect on the investment of the limited partner. The limited investor could potentially lose their investment, all because of poor management and poor business decision-making.

The reason why someone would choose an LP varies, from lack of managerial skills in the industry (yet money to invest, due to seeing an opportunity for profit and growth) to someone who has been in the industry for many years but has no interest in managing anymore. They just want the investment and they know the game. In the case of the gym, the silent partner had been in the gym business for decades, and he owned several gyms in different locations and sold them off. This particular gym he kept, but only as a silent partner. He allowed the other partner to buy into the business and be the general partner in the partnership.

Again, there is also the **limited liability partnership (LLP)**. According to the SBA, "*limited liability partnerships are similar to limited partnerships but give limited liability to every owner. An LLP protects each partner from debts against the partnership, and they won't be responsible for the actions of other partners.*"[14]

As a final reminder regarding partnerships, you are getting into bed with someone, as they say. Be cautious. Cover your bases. Make sure everything is in writing and that you have a clear escape clause. Seek legal counsel. Then go roll around in the hay and see if you can make some magic. With partners, we are stronger. We have combined resources, talents, skills, and abilities. Partnerships are known to have nice business lifespans. When done right, partnerships are the stones on which to build a very secure and stable foundation. Two are greater than one, for they have double the labor. And if either falls, the other is there to pick him or her up.

Now on to a **limited liability company** (LLC). According to the SBA website, "*an LLC lets you take advantage of the benefits of both the corporation and partnership business structures. LLCs protect you from personal liability in most instances, your personal assets—like your vehicle, house, and sav-*

ings accounts—won't be at risk in case your LLC faces bankruptcy or lawsuits. Profits and losses can get passed through to your personal income without facing corporate taxes. However, members of an LLC are considered self-employed and must pay self-employment tax contributions towards Medicare and Social Security.

LLCs can have a limited life in many states. When a member joins or leaves an LLC, some states may require the LLC to be dissolved and reformed with new membership—unless there's already an agreement in place within the LLC for buying, selling, and transferring ownership.

LLCs can be a good choice for medium- or higher-risk businesses, owners with significant personal assets they want to be protected, and owners who want to pay a lower tax rate than they would with a corporation."[14]

Today, LLCs seem to be very popular. Many times, I have had students and clients come to me who have already formed their business as an LLC. There is a process to filing an LLC. Below you find that I have provided the steps you need to follow. I just want you to understand that this is a very common form of business, as it does protect the business owner from the business itself. You will want to work with an attorney or lawyer when forming your business if you specifically plan to form yourself as an LLC.

According to Nolo, here are some steps that you can take to form an LLC:

1. "***Choose an LLC name.*** *The name of your business cannot be the same as the name of another limited liability company (LLC) on file with your state's LLC office (which is usually part of the same division as corporations, often the Secretary of State's office). The name must end with an LLC designator, such as "Limited Liability Company" or "Limited Company," or an abbreviation of one of these phrases ("LLC," "L.L.C.," or "Ltd. Liability Co.").*

2. ***File articles of organization.*** *Prepare and file "articles of organization" with your state's LLC filing office. Typically, you must provide only your LLC's name, its address, and sometimes the names of all of the owners—called members.*

3. Create an LLC operating agreement. *The LLC operating agreement contains rules for the ownership and operation of the business (much like a partnership agreement or corporate bylaws). A typical operating agreement includes the members' percentage interests in the business, the members' rights and responsibilities, and information on voting, management, and profits and losses.*

4. Publish a notice (AZ and NY only). *This step does not apply to LLCs in most states. If you are forming an LLC in Arizona or New York, you must take an additional step to make your company official: You must publish in a local newspaper a notice stating that you intend to form an LLC. Your local newspaper should be able to help you with this filing.*

5. Obtain licenses and permits. *Before you begin doing business, you need to obtain the required licenses and permits that anyone needs to start a new business. Among the licenses and permits you may need to obtain are a business license and, if your LLC will sell products, a seller's permit.*

6. Retain your limited liability. *To retain your LLC's status as a separate entity, LLC owners (members) must observe certain formalities, such as keeping detailed financial records and recording minutes of major decisions."*[15]

The following information comes directly from the SBA. A ***corporation (C corp)*** is "*a legal entity that's separate from its owners. Corporations can make a profit, be taxed, and can be held legally liable. Corporations offer the strongest protection to their owners from personal liability, but the cost to form a corporation is higher than other structures. Corporations also require more extensive record-keeping, operational processes, and reporting. Unlike sole proprietors, partnerships, and LLCs, corporations pay income tax on their profits. In some cases, corporate profits are taxed twice—first, when the company makes a profit, and again when dividends are paid to shareholders on their personal tax returns. Corporations have a completely independent life separate from their shareholders. If a shareholder leaves the compa-*

ny or sells his or her shares, the C corp can continue doing business relatively undisturbed. Corporations have an advantage when it comes to raising capital because they can raise funds through the sale of stock, which can also be a benefit in attracting employees. Corporations can be a good choice for medium- to higher-risk businesses, or businesses that need to raise money, and businesses that plan to 'go public' or eventually to be sold.

S corp. *An S corporation, sometimes called an S corp, is a special type of corporation that's designed to avoid the double taxation drawback of regular C corps. S corps allow profits, and some losses, to be passed through directly to owners' personal income without ever being subject to corporate tax rates. Not all states tax S corps equally, but most recognize them the same way the federal government does and taxes the shareholders accordingly. Some states tax S corps on profits above a specified limit and other states don't recognize the S corp election at all, simply treating the business as a C corp. S corps must file with the IRS to get S corp status, a different process from registering with their state. There are special limits on S corps. S corps can't have more than 100 shareholders, and all shareholders must be U.S. citizens. You'll still have to follow the strict filing and operational processes of a C corp. S corps also have an independent life, just like C corps. If a shareholder leaves the company or sells his or her shares, the S corp can continue doing business relatively undisturbed. S corps can be a good choice for a business that would otherwise be a C corp, but meet the criteria to file as an S corp.*

B corp. *A benefit corporation, sometimes called a B corp, is a for-profit corporation recognized in the majority of U.S. states. B corps are different from C corps in purpose, accountability, and transparency, but aren't different in how they're taxed. B corps are driven by both mission and profit. Shareholders hold the company accountable to produce some sort of public benefit in addition to a financial profit. Some states require B corps to submit annual benefit reports that demonstrate their contribution to the public good. There are several third-party B corp certification services, but none are re-*

quired for a company to be legally considered a B corp in a state where the legal status is available.

Close corporation. *Close corporations resemble B corps but have a less traditional corporate structure. These shed many formalities that typically govern corporations and apply to smaller companies. State rules vary, but shares are usually barred from public trading. Close corporations can be run by a small group of shareholders without a board of directors.*

Nonprofit corporation. *Nonprofit corporations are organized to do charity, education, religious, literary, or scientific work. Because their work benefits the public, nonprofits can receive tax-exempt status, meaning they don't pay state or federal taxes income taxes on any profits they make. Nonprofits must file with the IRS to get tax exemption, a different process from registering with their state. Nonprofit corporations need to follow organizational rules very similar to a regular C corp. They also need to follow special rules about what they do with any profits they earn. For example, they can't distribute profits to members or political campaigns. Nonprofits are often called 501(c)(3) corporations—a reference to the section of the Internal Revenue Code that is most commonly used to grant tax-exempt status.*

Cooperative. *A cooperative is a business or organization owned by and operated for the benefit of those using its services. Profits and earnings generated by the cooperative are distributed among the members, also known as user/owners. Typically, an elected board of directors and officers run the cooperative while regular members have voting power to control the direction of the cooperative. Members can become part of the cooperative by purchasing shares, though the number of shares they hold does not affect the weight of their vote."*[14]

Is your head spinning? Are you still perplexed as to which business legal structure to choose? Don't worry. Business structures have a lot of moving parts. Take my advice and find a small business lawyer to help you. If you don't have the money for legal help, I would suggest reaching out to the closest law school. Many law schools have free law clinics. The students, in my opinion, are fresher than some lawyers, and they are more eager to learn. See what advice they offer you. Deciding your legal structure is very important and you really do need to make the best decision. As I stated in the beginning, you will need to assess your risk and how much you have in assets that could be lost if some legal matter does come up.

You are able to change your business structure along the way, so if starting as a sole proprietor is the wisest choice, then go with it. Then, as you grow in assets and your business grows in risk, you will be able to consider restructuring your business. What I don't want you to do is jump into an LLC, pay large sums of money, and end up on the losing side.

In the back of the book, I have provided a chart that lays out all the different types of business structures we just covered.

Business Legal Structure Activity

Understanding the different legal structures for businesses is one of the most complex parts to learning business. Time and time again, I see students struggle to not only understand, but they struggle with knowing which legal structure to select. You must consider all your risks. As a sole proprietor, you are 100% responsible for all liabilities, as you and the business are one. When you are a Limited Liability Company (LLC) or Corporation (C Corp, S Corp), the liability is on the business, not you. You will need your book next to you as you work on this next activity to help you better understand how to structure your business. In this activity, you are going to be given a series of scenarios, and you will need to select the business structure that best fits.

1. John and Ryan have been friends since high school and even attended college together. Ryan graduated with a degree in computer science. John earned a degree in business administration. Both have an interest in computers. They have been helping family and friends since high school with minor computer issues. They notice that in their local town, no one is providing computer services. They each have some savings and are considering going into business. What legal structure should

they choose? When choosing that legal structure, what are things they need to consider and have in place? What are the pros and cons of the legal structure chosen?

_____
_____
_____
_____
_____
_____
_____
_____

2. Racheal is a stay-at-home mom. She and her family have successfully eliminated over $60,000 in debt, and she is gifted in what one would call "mom economics." Racheal took a night college class in small business management to explore options for starting her own business. Her college professor encouraged her to build a business based on her removal of debt and her "mom economics." She has low risk and few personal assets, but she does own a home. In what business legal structure should Rachael form her business? What will she need to do in order to form her business in this legal structure? What are the pros and cons of forming her business with the legal structure chosen?

_____
_____
_____
_____
_____
_____
_____
_____

3. Margret sells specialized soaps and lotions that she makes in-house. She has a growing client list and a thriving business. She is currently a sole proprietor but feels the need to change her business legal structure. What would you advise her to do? What next legal structure do you believe would be her best fit? What would she need to consider when selecting the chosen legal structure? What are the pros and cons of the chosen structure?

_____
_____
_____
_____
_____
_____
_____
_____
_____
_____

4. Byron owns a family business that was passed down to him from his grandfather. The business, founded in 1959, is a retail paint store that also specializes in window installations. The business started as a sole proprietorship; then, in early 1980, it changed to a limited liability company. Byron is considering changing the legal structure. The business is thriving, and growth potential is very high. The family already owns three locations, and more are on the horizon. Which legal structure would you advise Byron to choose? What would he need to consider when selecting the chosen legal structure? What are the pros and cons of the chosen structure?

_____
_____
_____
_____

Now I want you to take some time and think about what legal structure would work best for you and your business. I need you to be realistic. If you don't have any assets, what are you really protecting? Remember, as a sole proprietor, you are responsible for all liability. But what are your risks? You need to carefully consider everything. I encourage you to take time to think and write what comes to you.

Intellectual Property

"To achieve patent commercialization success, every inventor must think like a businessman."

—Kalyan C. Kankanala, IP attorney

Each of us has intellectual property (IP). IP is an asset to an individual, and many businesses thrive off of IP. I remember all too well my state job interview. In the third and final interview, I politely stated that I had intellectual property available for lease. The interviewers looked at each other and then looked at me. I'm not exactly sure what their thoughts were, but I received a call no sooner than I made it home, telling me I was hired and that I started on the Tuesday following Labor Day. Boom! I was in, just like that. IP sealed the deal. I gave the state quite a bit of my IP until enough was enough. Now I am very protective of my IP, and you should be as well. As a startup, you will be creating new products and services. IP covers everything from actual creation of those products to the creation of systems and much more.

There are four major types of IP:

- A **copyright** gives the creator of an original work exclusive rights to it, usually for a limited time. Copyright may apply to a wide range of creative, intellectual, or artistic forms, or works. Copyright does not cover ideas and information themselves, only the form or manner in which they are expressed. The life of a copyright lasts the lifetime of the artist/author's life plus 70 years.
- A **trademark** is a recognizable sign, design, or expression which distinguishes products or services of a particular trader from the similar products or services of other traders. Trademarks last 10 years and are able to be renewed.

- A **trade secret** is a formula, practice, process, design, instrument, pattern, or compilation of information that is not generally known or reasonably ascertainable, by which a business can obtain an economic advantage over competitors and customers. There is no formal government protection granted; each business must take measures to guard its own trade secrets (e.g., formula of its soft drinks is a trade secret for Coca-Cola).
- A **patent** is a form of right granted by the government to an inventor or their successor-in-title, giving the owner the right to exclude others from making, using, selling, offering to sell, and importing an invention for a limited period of time, in exchange for the public disclosure of the invention. An invention is a solution to a specific technological problem, which may be a product or a process and generally has to fulfill three main requirements: it has to be new, not obvious, and there needs to be an industrial applicability. The patent will have a life span of 20 years from the filing date.

Just as there are costs to forming your business, there are costs to protecting your IP. You definitely want to hire an attorney who works specifically with IP. Do not risk going to one who doesn't—you may end up not just losing your IP, but a lot of money, too.

Intellectual Property Search Activity

For this activity, you will need access the web so you can do a patent and trademark search. You will find the patent and trademark search on the same website: https://www.uspto.gov/.[16] You will go to that website and start with a patent search. Then you will do a trademark search. I also encourage you to read over the information on the site. Explore the site, not just the search option.

1. Patent search: What do you own that you just love? I want you to go to the site and do a patent search on that item. Pay attention to what you

find. Read all sections, as there is a lot of information given. Now go and do a search for something related to your business. What did you find? Make sure to note all that you found.

2. Now I want you to do a trademark search. You can trademark words as well as logos. Go do a search again for a product that you know. Nike, for example. Go check out the trademark information on Nike or another brand you love. Then I want you to search a trademark for your business name and see what comes up. Write down all that you find.

Be sure to seek legal counsel or even an accountant before you make any decisions on how you will form your business and how best to protect your IP. Take the time to make the right decision now so you do not end up losing in the future. Do not operate out of FEAR. Instead, make an educated and realistic decision. Remember, you are an empowered entrepreneur!

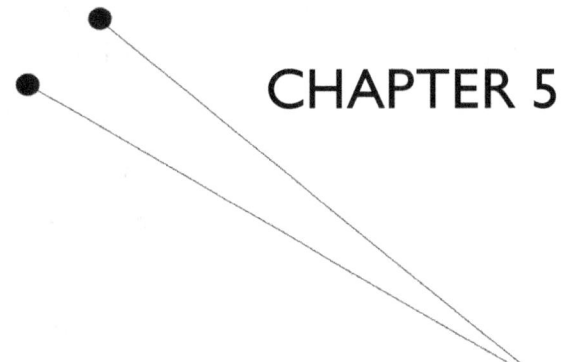

CHAPTER 5

DBA, EIN, Bank Account, and Business Insurance

"There is no finish line. There are only mile markers."

—Michael Ventura, CEO and founder of Sub Rosa

I want you to remember the above quote as you travel through your journey from startup to success. Mile markers are goals and things to get done. They are all part of your project management system, which we covered in Chapter 2. I called them milestones. Mile markers and milestones are the same concept. They are key in execution. In the previous chapter, you read all about how to legally structure your business and how to properly protect your intellectual property. I want you to learn all you can about both. I want you to seek the wisdom of others who are qualified to help you make the best decisions. I am now going to share more mile markers that you will need to help you accomplish your goals. You may not need all of them, but you will need some of them.

You will need to be sure that you have not only a business structure selected, but also a business name to be registered. For me, the business I bought had a name. All I needed to do was register that I was now doing business as (DBA) Start To Finish Files. If you purchase a business that has an existing name, you will need to do the same. Once you get your DBA (**D**oing **B**usiness **A**s; see below), you will then be able to open a bank account in the business name, which is very important. I will cover more on this later. First, there are four ways to register your name:

1. Entity name
2. Trademark
3. Doing Business As (DBA) name
4. Domain name

The following information comes directly from the SBA: "*An entity name can protect the name of your business at a state level. Depending on your business structure and location, the state may require you to register a legal entity name. Your entity name is how the state identifies your business. Each state may have different rules about what your entity name can be and usage of company suffixes. Most states don't allow you to register a name that's already been registered by someone else, and some states require your entity name to reflect the kind of business it represents. In most cases, your entity name registration protects your business and prevents anyone else in the state from operating under the same entity name. However, there are exceptions pertaining to state and business structure. Check with your state for rules about how to register your business name.*

A trademark can protect the name of your business, goods, and services at a national level. Trademarks prevent others in the same (or similar) industry in the U.S. from using your trademarked names. For example, if you were an electronics company and wanted to call your business Springfield Electronic Accessories and one of your products Screen Cover 5000, trademarking those names would prevent other electronics businesses or similar products from using those same names. Businesses in every state are subject to trademark infringement lawsuits, which can prove costly. That's why you should check your prospective business, product, and service names against the official trademark database, maintained by the United States Patent and Trademark Office.

You might need to register your DBA—also known as a trade name, fictitious name, or assumed name—with the state, county, or city your business is located in. Registering your DBA name doesn't provide legal protection by itself, but most states require you to register your DBA if you use one. Some business structures require you to use a DBA. Even if you're not required to register a DBA, you might want to anyway. A DBA lets you conduct business under a different identity from your own personal name or your formal business entity name. As an added bonus, getting a DBA and federal tax ID number (EIN) allows you to open a business bank account. Multiple businesses can go by the same DBA in one state, so you're less restricted in what you can choose. There's also more leeway in the clarity of business function. For example, a small business owner could use Springfield Electronic Accessories for their entity name but use TechBuddy for their DBA. Just remember that trademark infringement laws will still apply. Determine your DBA requirements based on your specific location. Requirements vary by business structure as well as by state, county, and municipality, so check with local government offices and websites.

If you want an online presence for your business, start by registering a domain name—also known as your website address, or URL. Once you register your domain name, no one else can use it for as long as you continue to own it. It's a good way to protect your brand presence online. If someone else has already registered the domain you wanted to use, that's okay. Your domain name doesn't actually need to be the same as your legal business name, trademark, or DBA. For example, Springfield Electronic Accessories could register the domain name techbuddyspringfield.com. You'll register your domain name through a registrar service. Consult a directory of accredited registrars to determine which ones are safe to use, and then pick one that offers you the best combination of price and customer service. You'll need to renew your domain registration on a regular basis.

The next part of launching your business is obtaining your Employer Identification Number (EIN), which is your federal tax ID. You need it to pay federal taxes, hire employees, open a bank account, and apply for business licenses and permits. It's free to apply for an EIN, and you should do it right after you register your business. Your business needs a federal tax ID number if it does any of the following:

- *Pays employees*
- *Operates as a corporation or partnership*
- *Files tax returns for employment, excise, or alcohol, tobacco, and firearms*
- *Withholds taxes on income, other than wages, paid to a non-resident alien*
- *Uses a Keogh Plan (a tax-deferred pension plan)*
- *Works with certain types of organizations*

Apply for an EIN with the IRS assistance tool. It will guide you through questions and ask for your name, social security number, address, and your 'Doing Business As' (DBA) name. Your nine-digit federal tax ID becomes available immediately upon verification.

Next comes the licenses and permits if needed. You'll need to get a federal license or permit if your business activities are regulated by a federal agency. Check to see if any of your business activities are listed here, and then check with the right federal agency to see how to apply. Requirements and fees depend on your business activity and the agency issuing the license or permit. It's best to check with the issuing agency for details on the business license cost. SBA gives you a beautiful chart that directs you where to go for permits. The licenses and permits you need from the state, county, or city will depend on your business activities and business location. Your business license fees will also vary.

States tend to regulate a broader range of activities than the federal government. For example, business activities that are commonly regulated locally include auctions, construction, and dry cleaning, farming, plumbing, restaurants, retail, and vending machines. Some licenses and permits expire after a set period of time. Keep close track of when you need to renew them—it's often easier to renew than it is to apply for a new one. You'll have to research your own state, county, and city regulations. Industry requirements often vary by state. Visit your state's website to find out which permits and licenses you need."[14]

To help you better understand what we have covered so far, I am giving you a few activities to do. You will find a series of questions to help guide you along the way. You will be doing research on a DBA and EIN. This information will help you, as you will need one or the other or perhaps both. I am providing you with space to write about what you find from doing your research.

1. Name search is done via the county clerk's or recorder's office. You will need to ensure no one else is using the name you have selected as your DBA. Of course, if it is taken, then you will need to select another name. With your name, please keep in mind that in California you will need to ensure you don't use Incorporated (Inc.), Corporation (Corp), or Limited Liability Corporation (LLC) if the business is not legally formed as one of those business structures in either California or another jurisdiction.
2. File appropriate paperwork with the county clerk or recorder's office and pay a filing fee.
3. Publish in a local paper that you are doing business as the name you have filed. This is required and must be done within 30 days of filing.

Those are the basic steps. Space has been provided for you to write what you find from your local county clerk's or recorder's office. Remember, a quick Google search will locate the contact information of the county office you need to contact.

If you plan to have employees, you are required by law to have an EIN. It is a very simple process. The following steps are how you file for and obtain an EIN. The following information comes directly off the IRS website[10] (see below). As I have stated before, I highly suggest you explore both the SBA and IRS websites as they will be one of your top resources in business.

1. "Determine Eligibility: You may apply for an EIN online if your principal business is located in the United States or U.S. Territories. The person applying online must have a valid Taxpayer Identification Number (SSN, ITIN, EIN). You are limited to one EIN per responsible party per day. The 'responsible party' is the person who ultimately owns or controls the entity or who exercises ultimate effective control over the entity. Unless the applicant is a government entity, the responsible party must be an individual (i.e., a natural person), not an entity."

2. Understand the Online Application: "You must complete this application in one session, as you will not be able to save and return at a later time. Your session will expire after 15 minutes of inactivity, and you will need to start over."

3. Submit Your Application: "After all validations are done, you will get your EIN immediately upon completion. You can then download, save, and print your EIN confirmation notice."

You see how simple that is. Now go to www.irs.gov[17] and search for EIN and then read all that you find. Make notes in the space provided. I suggest you even click on the apply button and take a peek at what the application looks like. Remember that the more knowledge you have, the more EMPOWERED you are!

_____

_____

_____

_____

You will also need to get a business bank account. As soon as you start accepting or spending money as your business, you should open a business bank account. Common business accounts include a checking account, savings account, credit card account, and a merchant services account. Merchant services accounts allow you to accept credit and debit card transactions from your customers. You can open a business bank account once you've gotten your federal EIN. Most business bank accounts offer perks that don't come with a standard personal bank account.

- Protection. Business banking offers limited personal liability protection by keeping your business funds separate from your personal funds. Merchant services also offer purchase protection for your customers and ensures that their personal information is secure.
- Professionalism. Customers will be able to pay you with credit cards and make checks out to your business instead of directly to you. Plus, you'll be able to authorize employees to handle day-to-day banking tasks on behalf of the business.
- Preparedness. Business banking usually comes with the option for a line of credit for the company. This can be used in the event of an emergency, or if your business needs new equipment.
- Purchasing power. Credit card accounts can help your business make large startup purchases and help establish a credit history for your business.

Opening a business bank account is easy once you've picked your bank. Simply go online or to a local branch to begin the process. Here are some of the most common documents banks ask for when you open a business bank account. Some banks may ask for more.

- Employer Identification Number (EIN) (or a Social Security number, if you're a sole proprietorship)
- Your business's formation documents
- Ownership agreements
- Business license

Make sure you are prepared when going to the bank to set up your account and, as always, do your research on which bank is best for you. Personally, I have my business account with a credit union. The man I bought my business from helped me set up my business account with Patelco Credit Union, and it has been a great place for all my banking needs in business and in my personal accounts. Do your research.

Business Bank Account

You are going to need a business bank account. It is important to keep your personal and business funds separate. Only use the business account for business. Don't mingle them together. That is bad for business. Once you have your DBA, you can take that to the bank and open a business bank account. You will also want to make sure to develop a professional business relationship with your banker. You will find in business that building relationships is mission-critical to the success of your business. You are now going to research banks and find out all you can regarding the business accounts at each bank. Remember, the more you find out, the better. Knowledge is power. In the space provided, write all that you find from your research.

_____
_____
_____
_____
_____
_____
_____
_____
_____
_____

You will also need to research the different types of insurance you will need to have. I do have a recommendation for a wonderful trustworthy insurance agent, Anthony Grigsby. When I work with clients, I send them to him for their insurance needs. It is important you have a knowledgeable insurance agent and one who is trustworthy. You will find Anthony's information in the back of the book.

Some industries require particular types of insurance, and without that type of insurance, you will not be able to conduct business. Make sure you know your industry and what is required. The following information comes directly from the SBA.

There are six common types of insurance:

1. "***General liability insurance***
    a. *Any business.*
    b. *This coverage protects against financial loss as the result of bodily injury, property damage, medical expenses, libel, slander, defending lawsuits, and settlement bonds or judgments.*
2. ***Product liability insurance***
    a. *Businesses that manufacture, wholesale, distribute, and retail a product.*
    b. *This coverage protects against financial loss as a result of a defective product that causes injury or bodily harm.*
3. ***Professional liability insurance***
    a. *Businesses that provide services to customers.*
    b. *This coverage protects against financial loss as a result of malpractice, errors, and negligence.*
4. ***Commercial property insurance***
    a. *Businesses with a significant amount of property and physical assets.*
    b. *This coverage protects your business against loss and damage of company property due to a wide variety of events such as fire, smoke, wind and hail storms, civil disobedience and vandalism.*

5. **Home-based business insurance**
   a. Businesses that are run out of the owner's personal home.
   b. Coverage that's added to homeowner's insurance as a rider can offer protection for a small amount of business equipment and liability coverage for third-party injuries.
6. **Business owner's policy**
   a. Most small business owners, but especially home-based business owners.
   b. A business owner's policy is an insurance package that combines all of the typical coverage options into one bundle. They simplify the insurance buying process and can save you money.

There are four steps to buying business insurance:
1. **Assess your risks**. Think about what kind of accidents, natural disasters, or lawsuits could damage your business. If you need help, the National Federation of Independent Businesses (NFIB) provides information for choosing insurance to help you assess your risks and to make sure you've insured every aspect of your business.
2. **Find a reputable licensed agent**. Commercial insurance agents can help you find policies that match your business needs. They receive commissions from insurance companies when they sell policies, so it's important to find a licensed agent that's interested in your needs as much as his/her own.
3. **Shop around**. Prices and benefits can vary significantly. You should compare rates, terms, and benefits for insurance offers from several different agents.
4. **Reassess every year**. As your business grows, so do your liabilities. If you have purchased or replaced equipment or expanded operations, you should contact your insurance agent to discuss changes in your business and how they affect your coverage."[14]

I would now like you to do some research on insurance. You can look for most commonly needed or used insurance for your industry. I want you to find out what the policy covers, how much the deductible is, what the cost of the insurance is, and then ask any other questions you can think of. In the space provided, write what you find from your research.

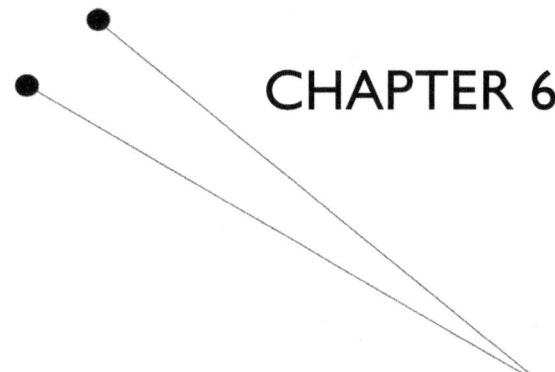

CHAPTER 6

Business Planning

"Planning is bringing the future into the present so that you can do something about it now."

—Alan Lakein, author

We are now going to begin our planning phase. The empowered entrepreneur understands that any plan is only black words on white paper, and if not brought to life by DOING, the plan is worthless. I am not a big believer in the business plan. I wrote one business plan in my life. I wrote it while earning my master's degree. By that point, I had already tripled my business. I believe business plans are outdated and irrelevant for today's aggressive and fast-moving market. They do not work best for startups. That being said, I do believe in planning. Plans are mission-critical; business plans have a place and time. I do work with clients all the time, helping them build business plans, but I always have them start with the business model canvas (BMC). The BMC is more commonly used in the startup word. They are more commonly used in the business world, period. You will be asked time and time again, what is your business model? Therefore, in this chapter you will find that the activities I have for you are geared toward working with the BMC and your pitch deck. Before we head there, I will give you some information on the traditional business plan. You will certainly need one if you are seeking a loan from the Small Business Administration (SBA) or one of its sister organizations.

The SBA backs 80% of small business loans. They are not the ones that give the loans out; they only back the loan. The banks loan the money to the lender. You must be credit-worthy in order to receive a loan. Please keep in mind, even existing businesses that have been in business for many years and have solid statistical data can be disqualified by the SBA. Your chances are much higher if you have excellent credit, and your personal and business finances are in good health. "*The SBA requires a personal guarantee from every owner with at least a 20% ownership stake and from others who hold top management positions. A personal guarantee puts you and your personal assets on the hook for payments if your business can't make them.*"[14] I encourage you to go to the SBA's website, www.sba.gov, and explore. It is one of your most valuable resources and has a never-ending wealth of information. They will show you a traditional business plan, and now they even have one that is a lean version.

The traditional business plan is 28 to 35 pages in length, plus appendices that include financial statements. The business plan is a series of several different types of analysis. It will have a cover page where the name of the business, the owner's name, and their contact information can be found. The next thing the reader sees is the table of contents. Business plans are lengthy. The table of contents helps the reader navigate the space. The executive summary is crucial to the business plan and is found directly after the table of contents. In the back of the book, I have provided a template of what a traditional business plan consists of.

My advice to you is that you seek out help when writing your plan. You will never take one class or go to a one-time workshop and come out some badass business plan writer. That is just not going to happen. It takes a lot of work to write a well-written business plan. And, in order to receive funding, you will need one that is well done. Therefore, I recommend you find someone who has been writing them and can help you. Your chances of getting funded are much higher with a well-written plan and solid data. To write or not to write a business plan is really up to you. Remember that if you are seeking a bank loan, you will most definitely need to write a business plan. If you are starting a business, however, you have other options available to you. We are now going to explore those options. I believe you will be pleasantly surprised to see how much more efficient and effective these more modern ways of planning are.

"Unless you are a fortune-teller, long-term business planning is a fantasy."

—Jason Fried, co-founder of 37signals

Allow me to introduce you to the business model canvas. This is the fundamental business tool that startups use in the building and planning phase of their businesses. The business model canvas is your new best friend. It starts as a business model, which has four key drivers: the offering, the customers, the infrastructure, and the financial viability.

INFRASTRUCTURE	OFFERING	CUSTOMERS
FINANCES		

Those four key drivers then expand into nine building blocks. Those nine building blocks are the foundation of going from startup to success.

What you will see in the next illustration is that the offering is the only thing that doesn't break down. The reason for that is the offering is your "purple cow," as we say in the business world. It is your value proposition statement. It is what sets you apart from all others. Your infrastructure will break down into three drivers: key partners, key activities, and key resources. Your customers will break down into three drivers as well: customer relationships, customer channels, and customer segments. The base of your model—finances—is broken in half: cost structure and revenue structure.

Key Partners	Key Activities	Value Proposition	Customer Relationships	Customer Segments
	Key Resources		Channels	
Cost Structure		Revenue Streams		

Both images were created by Entrepreneurship Empowered based on Alexander Osterwalder, Business Model Generation

The offering, which is also called the value proposition, is the most important part of your business model. Your job is to provide the most value you can to your customers and clients and the market you serve. You should be offering better value than your competitors, and you should be able to have sustainability, meaning you must be able to execute on your value for a length of time. The value proposition solves problems and relieves pain.

Now how do we get the job done to solve those problems? Because, in the end, the value you offer is directly tied to getting the job done. Cases will vary from customer to customer and business to business. You will need to understand your customer, who, many times, will let you know what job needs to be done, but whose needs you will also be uncovering. You are going to provide solutions, and you need to remember that your value should be the better solution for customers.

Customers face all kinds of problems in the new millennium. Those problems help guide you in creating solutions. There are four problems that stand out, and if you could address even one of the four, you could be set for life. Those four problems are lack of time, lack of money, lack of skills, and lack of access.

The internet has provided a wagon full of solutions for the lacks listed above. Take access, for example. Say you love Macy's, but you live far away from one. All you need to do is hop on the computer, go to the Macy's website, and shop for as long as your heart desires. You can shop in your pajamas and no one will look at you strangely. You can shop in the middle of the night and no one is going to wonder how you were able to get into the store after closing. The reason is that you brought the store to you. Lack of access, be gone!

The great thing about a business model canvas is that it allows you to easily and draw pictures or words about what your idea entails. It gives you a greater understanding of your business, and it helps develop a process of making connections to your ideas and converting those ideas into a business. It is a very useful tool to lay it all out. Then you develop further—you expand each of the nine building blocks to a deep level, which will help you as you begin to launch or grow your business. But again, remember the plan is no good on paper. You must bring it to life. You must execute the plan.

Business Model Canvas Brainstorming

For this activity, you are going to take time and think. Please answer each section of the business model canvas.

Customer Value Proposition (CVP)/Offering: (Note: this is your purple cow and what sets you apart from the rest.) What problem are you helping solve for your client or customer?

_____
_____
_____
_____
_____
_____
_____
_____
_____
_____

Customer Segments: Who are your customers? Who are the most important customers? The more detailed you can be with your customer segment, the better you will be able to market to them.

_____
_____
_____
_____
_____
_____
_____
_____

Channels: How are you going to communicate, distribute, and sell to your customers? Which way do they prefer? What are the most cost-effective channels? What are the most time-effective channels?

_____
_____
_____
_____
_____
_____
_____
_____
_____

Customer Relations: What way(s) will you get and keep new customers? How does this strategy fit in with the other parts of the business model?

_____
_____
_____
_____
_____
_____
_____
_____
_____

Key Resources: What do you need in order to offer your CVP?

_____
_____

Key Activities: What will you need to do in order to provide your CVP?

Key Partnerships: Who all will you need in order to deliver on your CVP? Who are your partners and suppliers? What things will you need to outsource to your partners? What resources do you need from your partner? Who is on your team?

Cost Structure: What are all of your costs involved in operating and running your business in order to fulfill your CVP?

Revenue Streams: What are your customers willing to pay? What do they currently pay for solving the problem? How many different revenue streams do you potentially have?

Moving on to our next major player: the feasibility study is used to test the possibilities of a new product, idea, or service. The study will show you if it is feasible for you to pursue the endeavor. A feasibility study could save you a lot of time, effort, and money when done correctly—because if your findings come back that your idea, product, or service is not feasible, you can shelve it until it could possibly be used. Or you could "can it" forevermore. What you don't want to end up doing is pursuing it only to find you have lost a ton of money. It is like climbing the corporate ladder only to discover that you have been climbing for twenty years up the wrong ladder—what a waste. The following elements are important to the feasibility study:

- *Does the idea fulfill a need or solve a big problem?*
- *Is there both a short- and long-term market potential?*
- *Who are the customers, and what are they willing to pay?*
- *Does the opportunity provide competitive uniqueness?*
- *Is the business model feasible (can it be done) and viable (can it be sustainable)?*

The formal study, when fully produced, will have a cover sheet, an executive summary (which you will want to write last), a technical and operational study, and a financial and resource study. You will need to ensure your market research is in there as well. The market research is mission-critical to all plans you put together. You will then close out with a final conclusion. We are going to dive deeper into market research and how to prepare a market plan in the upcoming chapter. As you can see, the market plan is actually a big piece of the feasibility study.

"Your pitch deck is your key to getting the dollar bills you need to give life to your business. Including the right content can mean the difference between walking out of your meeting a couple hundred thousand (or a couple million) dollars richer...or walking out with a firm handshake, a 'thanks but no thanks,' and a free coffee mug...if you're lucky."

—Deanna deBara, freelance writer and entrepreneur

The pitch deck is your showstopper and has been used to secure millions of dollars from investors. The pitch deck is a slide presentation that usually serves as a starting point to build off of by using the business model canvas. It will tell your target audience the key essentials of your business. More importantly, it starts by addressing what the problem is and what solution you have that fixes the problem. So, when it comes to creating the perfect pitch deck, where do you start? According to Design Shack, great pitch decks have several things in common:

- "***Consistent and error-free design***: *Slides in the pitch deck must look like they belong together with a professional look and design that is free of errors. (Proofread it twice!)*
- ***Something to hook the audience***: *Tell a story with words and visuals that engage people and make them want to be a part of your startup. You need to inspire them.*
- ***Value proposition***: *What makes your company special, unique and valuable? What should investors expect as a return? Spell it out.*
- ***Personality***: *A pitch deck should reflect your brand identity and personality.*
- ***Template***: *Don't reinvent the wheel every time you need to tweak or give your presentation to someone else. Create a template for your pitch deck (we have a few ideas below to help you get started and throughout this article) so that it's quick and easy to prepare a presentation on the fly. You never know where the right opportunity might be waiting.*"[18]

Pitch Deck Search Activity

There are many templates out there to use, and Guy Kawasaki is very well known for pitch decks and has several templates to review and use. Right now, google "Guy Kawasaki pitch decks." You are looking for the top ten slides that Guy recommends you'll need for your pitch deck. I want you to write those ten slides in the space provided below. Also, be sure to note any other suggestions he has for you regarding the presentation. Then, explore the templates he provides, and make sure to save a few for future reference. Take note of design elements, as well as content. This will help you as you develop your own pitch deck.

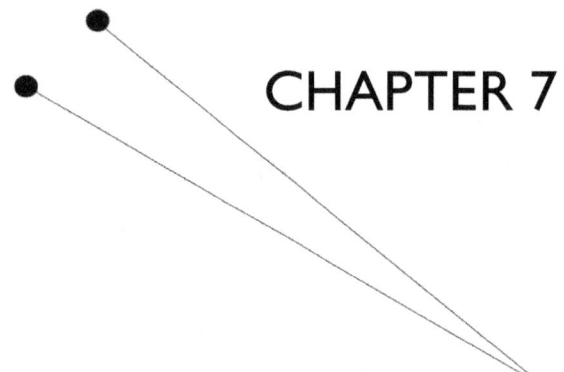

CHAPTER 7

Effective Communication

"Communication—the human connection—is the key to personal and career success."

—Paul J. Meyer, author and speaker

Communication is at the core of everything we do. We are constantly communicating, even when we are sleeping. In the jungle, the animals all speak different languages. This is why it is critical that you understand not only what type of animal you are, but also how to speak with the other animals in the jungle. A person who has the traits of a turtle is going to want all the details. They are going to want you to open up as much as you possibly can, and then they are going to want more. A lion, on the other hand, will get very pissed off if you give them too many details and do not get right to the point. They are only concerned with the point. What the hell is the point?! In business and in life, you are going to need to master communication.

According to Merriam-Webster, **communication** is defined as "*a process by which information is exchanged between individuals through a common system of symbols, signs, or behavior.*" Business communication is used for a wide variety of activities including, but not limited to: strategic communications planning, media relations, public relations (which can include social media, broadcast and written communications, and more), brand management, reputation management, speech writing, customer-client relations, and internal employee communications.

There are different types of communication, too. We will cover the top four: nonverbal, verbal, written, and visual. A business dictionary defines **nonverbal communication** as "*behavior and elements of speech aside from the words themselves that transmit meaning. Non-verbal communication includes pitch, speed, tone and volume of voice, gestures and facial expressions, body posture, stance, and proximity to the listener, eye movements and contact, and dress and appearance.*" We communicate nonverbally more often than we do verbally. Dr. Albert Mehrabian, author of *Silent Messages*, conducted several studies on nonverbal communication. He found that 7% of any message is conveyed through words, 38% through certain vocal elements, and 55% through nonverbal elements (facial expressions, gestures, posture, etc.).[19] Subtracting the 7% actual vocal content leaves one with 93%. Statistically speaking, 93% of communication is nonverbal. Can you believe that?

You need to understand that everything about you communicates—from the way you dress, to how you smell, to what comes out of your mouth, to how you listen. This is why it is important to take good care of yourself. I am always striving to become better than I was yesterday. Personal growth is very important to me, and I would encourage you to keep personal growth at the forefront of your mind. With regard to clothing, especially in business, you want to make sure you keep a professional look. This doesn't mean you need to wear a dress, a pantsuit, or a suit and tie all the time. It does, however, mean that you need to be presentable and have a clean appearance.

You need to smell good. I can promise you this much, you don't have to be rich to dress well and smell good. Any thrift store in town has quality clothing at a discounted rate. You just need to go look. There are also several nonprofit organizations that offer professional clothing to those who are in need, and they offer it for free. I share this with you because I understand what it is like to not have a lot of money. But style and class I have always had, with or without money. As far as smell goes, a nice bath, brushing of the teeth, and deodorant should be enough. You don't want to wear too much perfume or cologne because the scent can be overpowering. A nice light scent should do the trick. When you look your best, you normally feel your best. This is another reason why you want to make sure you are always dressing to impress, even if it is just you that you're impressing.

Verbal communication is defined as "*the sharing of information between individuals by using speech. Individuals working within a business need to effectively use verbal communication that employs readily understood spoken words, as well as ensuring that the enunciation, stress and tone of voice with which the words are expressed is appropriate.*" Communication, just as with many things in life, starts on the inside. Remember, *the way out is within*. You must be comfortable with yourself to effectively communicate with others. How do you communicate with yourself? What things are you saying to yourself?

Intrapersonal communication is also known as self-talk. Self-talk can be either positive or negative. For many years, I suffered with horrible self-talk. I would wander, far more than I care to admit, in the forest of falsehood and just sit under a tree of lies. Fatigued from my travels and all I carried, I would just sit and weep as the tree continually dropped lie after lie.

Then, I finally got up and became *EMPOWERED*. I took the keys to my life back, and I changed the way I communicated. First and foremost, with myself. Upon doing so, I worked on becoming a better communicator. I learned how to draw with my words. You will see me do it many times in this book. For me, communicating verbally means I need to show my story, not tell it. I need to bring it to life. It also means that I need to be authentic and real with those I am communicating with. In business, we are communicators, and we must be effective in order to go from startup to success.

Because we live in a digital age, where text and email have taken over so much, being able to verbally communicate well is sought after. My son once had a girlfriend who, in person, would hardly say a word. But boy oh boy, in a text, she would damn near write a book. She was far more comfortable behind the mask of the text than in person. I need you to be comfortable in person and virtually. In business, you will be required to be personable and communicate effectively in both realms. Your verbal communication is looked at today as a skill and a strength. If you want to learn to be a better verbal communicator, I encourage you to start by listening to some of the great verbal communicators. Our former president, Barack Obama, is an amazing verbal communicator. You can start by listening to some of his speeches. Even if you don't agree with his politics, you can know him for the power in which he speaks. Some other great verbal communicators include Nelson Mandela, John F. Kennedy, Martin Luther King, Jr., and Mahatma Gandhi.

The other way to become a better verbal communicator is to read. Reading was a struggle for a long time for me. I suffer from a minor form of dyslexia. I have an aunt who has full-blown dyslexia. She is unable to read or write. I have worked extremely hard to overcome my disability. I did this by first slowing down. I can move too fast. I learned that I would need to read over things several times to truly understand and comprehend them. I continued to read more and more and actually started to love reading. The more I read, the stronger I became and the less I suffered with comprehension. Imagine that. Practice not only makes perfect, it makes prepared. All the time I spent reading has helped me not only in my ability to read, but also my ability to write. The more I gathered words as I read, the stronger a communicator I became. My vocabulary increased, and even today, I continue to increase my vocabulary.

As speakers, one of the tools we use to help us grow is notecards with words on them. I suggest you give it a try. Just get yourself a stack of index cards. Pull out the dictionary and write the word and definition on the card. Pull out as many words as possible, then practice. Stand in front of the mirror and pull out a card, then create something to say around that word. Repeat as much as you need.

The other way to increase your ability to speak is to get out and start talking to people. As an empowered entrepreneur, networking is mandatory. In order to network, you are going to need to be able to communicate. You will need to communicate your core message regarding your business and your future. You need to communicate in such a way that your audience can understand what you are saying, and that you are able to provide for them what they need. There are many different types of networking events in your local area right now. All you have to do is search for them. If you are in my class at one of the colleges or my virtual course, you will be exposed to many different networking events, and I will ask you to attend a few of them. For now, I want you to find one on your own and go check it out. Just be observant and watch everyone communicating. Then, join in on the fun. Make sure to take a business card with you, even it just has your name and contact information on it. Remember, you don't need to have a business or fancy title to have a business card. You just need a name, number, and email. That's it. Your business card will serve as your visual and written communication.

Let's now turn our attention to the final two types of communication: written and visual.

Being a reader, I have already told you, was a struggle for me at first. I literally failed third grade because of it. However, as you can see, you are currently reading one of my books. I will write at least twenty to thirty books in my lifetime. Tell me again I am a failure. I promise I am coming for everything they told me I couldn't have.

Written communication involves anything using the written word to communicate a message. We have vast amounts of written communication.

This very book is written communication. In business, you will do a lot of writing. If you struggle with writing, I need you to take a writing course and grow as a writer. As an empowered entrepreneur, you are going to need to be an effective communicator, and writing is a large part of business. Written communication is one of the most common forms of business communication in the new millennium and will only increase as we move forward in time. When I first started teaching at the college level, I was shocked at how many students came out of high school and into college without knowing how to read or write well.

What the hell is really going on? How is it that our education system is failing our students like this? Those were my first questions. My next thought was, *How can I help correct it?* The first thing I did was expose my truth, just as I have done here with you. There is great freedom when we expose our truth because there is always someone in the valley ahead of us that needs our help. They need us to come to them and help raise them up. After that, I told each of my students that I would work directly with them, one on one, to help them become better writers. I gave them tools and tips on how to grow as a reader and a writer. Most importantly, I gave them work to do. Because they are going to have to write, I need them to write well. I am not just building up any type of entrepreneurs, I am building up *EMPOWERED* ones.

We only get better by practice. In order to master something, you must put in at least 10,000 hours. This is true with writing. I am very proud of this book, but the one I will write at my 10,000 mark—oh boy, that one you certainly need to buy. It is going to blow your socks off. Of this I am sure.

So, practice. Learn sentence structure and grammar and the like. The way to start your practice is to journal. Put your pen to paper and just write. Move the self-censoring out of the way and write what comes to you freely. Then go back over it. I still need an editor today. That is perfectly fine. You will want someone to proofread your work. There is nothing wrong with asking for help. Just don't allow others to do all the work for you. Make it a team effort.

The need to develop good writing skills is only highlighted by the fact that, in the new millennium, it is not uncommon to conduct business with customers and suppliers that are established and maintained exclusively through the use of written communications. Let's start with how to properly compose an email. First, you need to remember that you are composing an email, not a text. Text language, such as WYD (what you doing) or LOL (laugh out loud), is not going to work. Please remember that. The following email etiquette tips come from an article written by Vivian Giang, entitled "7 Email Etiquette Rules Every Professional Should Know." These tips originally appeared in Barbara Pachter's book, *The Essentials of Business Etiquette*.

- *"Use a professional email address*
- *Include a clear, direct subject line*
- *Include a salutation when starting an email stream, which can be left out when you are in the middle of a series of emails*
- *Formal: Dear Mr. Smith/Ms. Smith,*
- *Less Formal: Hello, John/Jane,*
- *Use the same sentence structure and paragraphs as in a letter, but you do not need to indent*
- *Try to stay short and to the point*
- *Create an email signature with your contact information, title, etc."* [20]

These tips are a great place to start, but there are some things I need you to remember not to do:

Be cautious when using the "reply all" button. At one of my colleges, the email system defaults to "reply all," and if you don't manually change it, you could easily respond to a group email and send your response to everyone. It can be such an inconvenience, not only to those who receive it, but also to the sender who really didn't need everyone to see their response.

Don't use ALL CAPS—that means you are yelling at someone. Remember, tone is not felt in words that are written. So, if you are trying to crack a joke, it may not be received as funny to the person on the other end. If you are sending something to a group of people, do them a favor and don't expose their email addresses unless it's necessary. Use a BCC, which stands for "blind cc." This way, you send the message to everyone without exposing their email addresses. You will need to send the email to yourself and then do the BCC for it to work.

The way you compose your email is very important, as well. Below are some examples of what to do and what not to do.

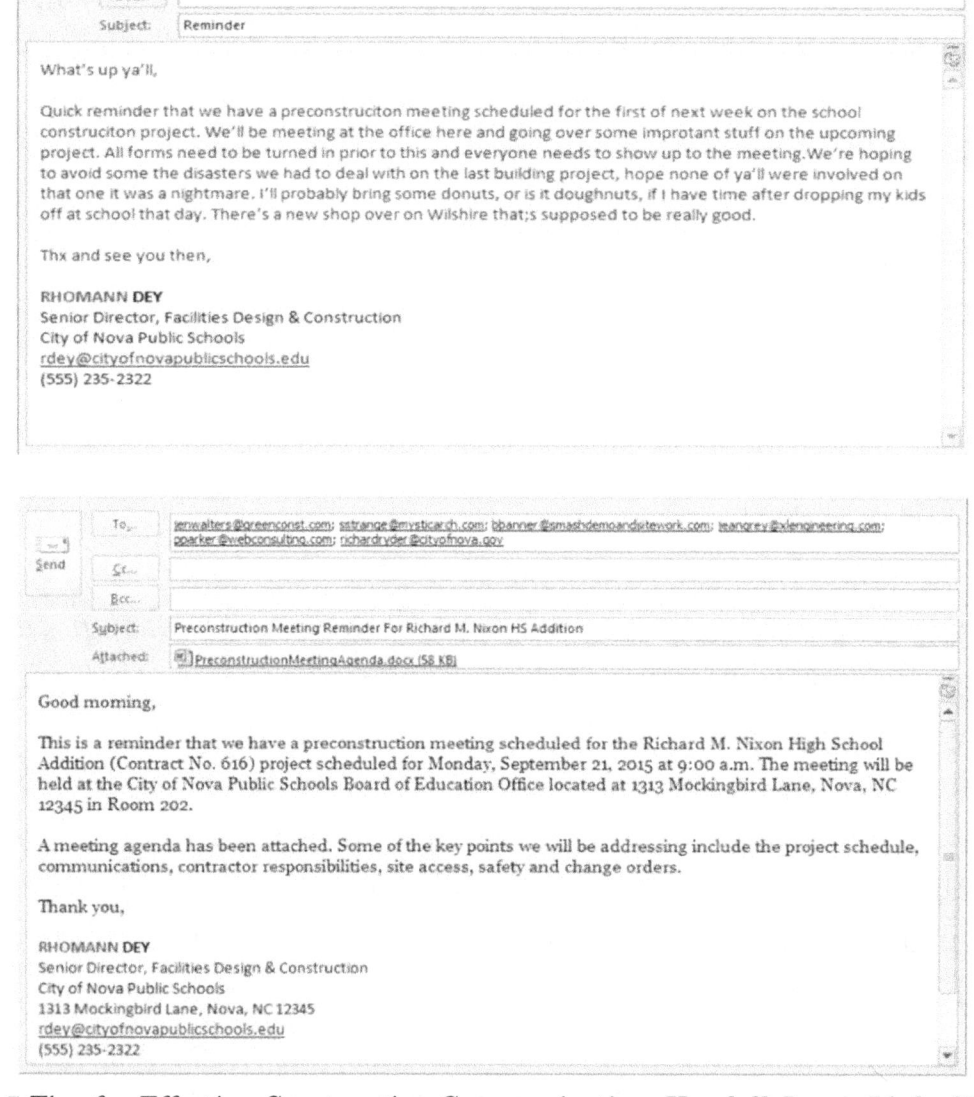

5 Tips for Effective Construction Communication, Kendall Jones, LinkedIn

Outside of emails, you will also need to be able to write memos and business reports. Memos are a little less formal, whereas business reports are more formal. Memos are very short messages. Business reports are four to five pages in length. They are fact-driven and will contain elements of research and a ton of data. They may have some opinions or recommendations, though. Business reports are widely used in corporations and larger-scale businesses. I am now going to leave you with some final tips on how to improve your business writing skills. The following tips come directly from an article written by Carolyn O'Hara, entitled "How to Improve Your Business Writing," published in the *Harvard Business Review*.

- "***Think before you write***—*Before you put pen to paper or hands to keyboard, consider what you want to say.* [Remember, it is all about the power of your mind. I need you to use all of it. —Natasha M Palumbo]
- ***Be direct***—*Make your point right up front. Many people find that the writing style and structure they developed in school doesn't work as well in the business world.* [Learn the language of the business world and use it to your advantage. —Natasha M Palumbo]
- ***Cut the fat***—*Read your writing through critical eyes, and make sure that each word works toward your larger point. Cut every unnecessary word or sentence.* [Remember, less is more. —Natasha M Palumbo]
- ***Avoid jargon and $10 words***—*Business writing is full of industry-specific buzzwords and acronyms. And while these terms are sometimes unavoidable and can occasionally be helpful as shorthand, they often indicate lazy or cluttered thinking. Throw in too many, and your reader will assume you are on autopilot—or worse, not understand what you're saying.* [Use your deck of cards. —Natasha M Palumbo]

- ***Read what you write**—Put yourself in your reader's shoes. Is your point clear and well-structured? Are the sentences straightforward and concise?* [Read out loud—it helps you hear what is wrong and what doesn't sound right. —Natasha M Palumbo]
- ***Practice every day**—Writing is a skill and skills improve with practice. Read well-written material every day, being attentive to word choice, sentence structure, and flow."*[21] [Practice makes perfect and prepared. —Natasha M Palumbo]

Merriam-Webster defines **visual communication** as "*any system of signaling in which the signals are received by the eye.*" In other words, visual communication in part or whole relies on eyesight. Visual communication is a broad spectrum that includes signs, typography, drawing, graphic design, illustration, industrial design, advertising, animation, color, and electronic resources.

We are by far more visual communicators in the new millennium than we have ever been before. As an educator, I am always using visual aids. I use PowerPoint slides for almost all of my lectures. They help give my students a better understanding of the information I am lecturing. As a speaker, I even use slides from time to time to help make my presentations more impactful. In business, I use a lot of visual communication. I have been creating flyers and brochures for close to fifteen years. They help me get my message out to potential and existing clients. You will want to ensure you are able to create some clean visuals for your business. Remember, the way you communicate should be a reflection of who you are.

You have now been given information on the four most common types of communication. But I want you to understand that what is most important is how you listen. You must be effective as a communicator to truly be an empowered entrepreneur. Effective communication requires you to listen—intently. Do not listen to respond, listen to understand. I learn so much from listening. I am a very observant person. My antennae are all the way up and I am always on the hunt for more knowledge. By listening, I can see things from a different perspective. This is why I tell my students and readers to go listen to some of the great speakers of our day, and even those of the past.

I also encourage you to ask questions when you are speaking with others. It is perfectly fine for someone to repeat something so you can fully understand them. This means you are listening with the intent to understand. It is also perfectly fine to take notes when you are at a meeting. That way, you can write down important pieces of the conversation. If you take one of my classes at the college or my virtual course online, I will go into more detail on how to be an effective communicator by listening. For now, I want you to keep your ears perked and your mind focused when communicating with others. I want you to become a master of communication. You will need to master this in life and in business, regardless of whether or not you are going to be an empowered entrepreneur. My goal in the end is to ensure that you are *EMPOWERED* and go from startup to success!

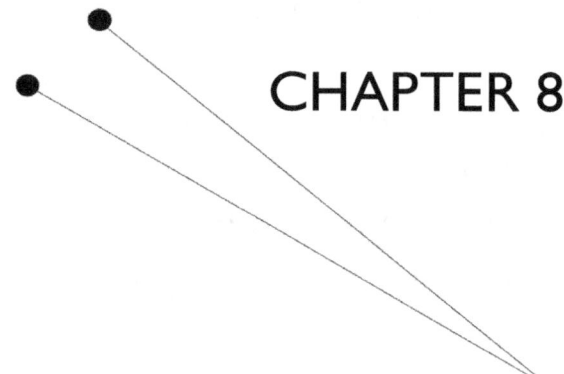

CHAPTER 8

Marketing and Branding

"It is very important to understand that emotional intelligence is not the opposite of intelligence, it is not the triumph of heart over head—it is the unique intersection of both."

—David Caruso, actor

Don't make marketing, make magic. Why do I say that, you ask? Well, because really good marketing is the best magic act you will ever see. You know how magic taps into our emotions? Well, that is what really good marketing does, too. Marketing should be tightly wrapped with emotional intelligence. Those who use emotional intelligence within marketing and business have great success and certainly greater profit. Take, for example, Proctor and Gamble (P&G). Their marketing team is absolutely genius with the use of emotional intelligence. During the World Olympics, they ran an ad that focused not on the star athletes, but rather the mothers. Mind you, the mothers are the target market for P&G. They are the buyers. The ad showcased how the mothers have always been there, taking the young athlete to practices, kissing their forehead after a bad game or poor performance, waving flags and cheering from the sidelines as the winning shot was scored. The entire time the ad was running, the most magical music played ever so softly in the background. Then, right as the ad came to a close, the most beautiful words appeared on the screen: **THANK YOU, MOM...** According to IGM Bizcuit, *"this one ad caused the brand attractiveness to grow by over 10%, and within a 17-day period of time the ad raked in 130 million dollars in sales."* Emotional intelligence is critical to marketing. If I am able to tug at your emotions, you had better believe I will easily grab your wallet with the best magic act on the strip. Emotional intelligence and color psychology go hand in hand. You are going to need to learn about both and use them in building your brand. I am now going to shift you into your first activity for this chapter.

Emotional Intelligence and Color Psychology

For this activity, you are going to do some research. I want you to find two or three articles on emotional intelligence—specifically in marketing. I also want you to check out how color is used. I want you to learn the psychology of color. I am providing you with a website to visit for color psychology. After you have done some research on emotional intelligence, I want you to find an emotional intelligence quiz and take it. See how emotionally intelligent you are. There are plenty of quizzes and assessments on the web for free that you can take. Then, in the space provided, I want you to write about what you found in your research. I also want you to think about how you are going to use emotional intelligence when creating your brand. I also want you to pick a color theme from the color psychology exercise and begin working with those colors as you develop your branding.

Link: https://www.colorpsychology.org/color-psychology-marketing/.[22]

_____

_____

_____

"Marketing is no longer about the stuff you sell, but the stories you tell."

—Seth Godin, author and entrepreneur

Marketing is one of my favorite pieces of the business puzzle. Marketing really is not just one piece to the puzzle, either. It's several pieces—each piece telling a different story. I see it as the border. You know how important the border is to a puzzle, right? Many people build the border first, then move on to filling in the other pieces to reveal the entire picture. Marketing is your border.

If you are going to go from startup to success, you must have a solid marketing plan. You will need to do market research and be wise in how you choose to brand your business. Your brand is your calling card, and you want to ensure the call is able to get through at all times. At no point should we be hearing you say, "Can you hear me now?" We must always be able to hear you. Your greatest marketing tool is word of mouth (WOM).

This takes me right back to emotional intelligence and its importance. You must be able to connect and relate to your customer or client. You must have empathy. Even more importantly, you must be making sure the job they need you to do is being done properly and in such a way that they have to tell everyone they know all about you and your business. The growth I saw in business was a direct result of WOM. Even today, the reason my classes fill up so fast is because of WOM. The reason this book will be flying off the shelves is because of WOM. The reason your business will boom is also because of WOM. So, understand how important WOM is, and be sure to include it in your marketing plan.

How do you build successful WOM marketing? You start with a foundation made of solid trust, commitment, and customer satisfaction. You make sure your customers or clients have some of your swag. T-shirts, coffee cups, pens, note pads...anything you can give to them to use which showcases your brand. Another way is to give a referral discount for sending new customers or clients your way. *"Bring a new customer and receive 10% off your next order!"* Or, better yet, give something away for FREE for the referral. According to academic research and Jonah Berger's bestselling book, *Contagious: Why Things Catch On,* there are six key factors that drive what people talk about and share. They are organized in an acronym called STEPPS, which stands for:

- "*Social Currency—the better something makes people look, the more likely they will be to share it*
- *Triggers—things that are top of mind (i.e., accessible) are more likely to be tip of tongue*
- *Emotion—when we care, we share. High-arousal emotions increase sharing*
- *Public—the easier something is to see, the more likely people are to imitate it*
- *Practical Value—people share useful information to help others*
- *Stories—Trojan Horse stories carry messages and ideas along for the ride"*[23]

If you recall the Muhammad Ali quote from Chapter 2, it closes with *sting like a bee*. Well, in WOM, part of your goal is to create a BUZZ like a BEE. This is where your marketing message is amplified by the public. Create an excitement around your product or service. I am now going to move us into branding and how to anchor yourself in your personal brand, so you build a business brand that outlasts you.

"All of us need to understand the importance of branding. We are CEOs of our own companies: Me Inc. To be in business today, our most important job is to be head marketer for the brand called You."

—Tom Peters, author

Branding is defined by the business dictionary as "*the process involved in creating a unique name and image for a product in the consumers' mind, mainly through advertising campaigns with a consistent theme. Branding aims to establish a significant and differentiated presence in the market that attracts and retains loyal customers."*

I need you to understand that your brand is a promise to your customers, letting them know what they can expect from your offering and how it is different from others. Your logo is the face of your brand. It is part of how you will communicate your brand message, and it should be seen everywhere to grow brand awareness.

The business dictionary defines brand strategy as *"the long-term marketing support for a brand, based on the definition of the characteristics of the target consumers. It includes an understanding of their preferences, and expectations from the brand."* This brand message will be seen through ads, distribution, and packaging. Two of the most powerful and classic brands are Coca-Cola, which has managed to differentiate itself from other sodas through its consistent strategic branding, and Nike, which involves famous athletes as part of its branding strategy.

When I work with students and clients, one the first things I have them do is this next activity that I'm going to have you do. You are the brand, and below is your self-branding assignment. I promise it will be a lot of fun. I'm all about anchoring you even deeper within yourself. Remember my quote: *"The way out is within."*

Self-Branding Exercise

I want you to ask five to seven people to describe you in three words. Tell them that you will not be upset by what they say if they did need to say something that could be a little hard to swallow. You need to know. Tell them not to think very long but say whatever three words come to mind. Make sure you write them down. If you see a word pop up more than once, make sure to circle that word. It may happen with a few words. Then you are going to reflect on what you have been told. The words that popped up a few times are your strongest brand traits. Now, do you agree or disagree with the way you were described? Write about it.

How people see you is your brand. You need to be aware of how you are being perceived. The next part of this assignment is to create a mantra or tagline. A mantra is short and to the point. This mantra is for your life. Not for a business, but for you. Then, the next step is to create a logo. Design yourself a personal logo. Remember the color psychology and be sure to pick personal brand colors that have meaning and align with who you are. I am going to provide you with examples of how I did this assignment, and then there will be space provided for you to write your answers. You may also want to use a computer to do this work.

Self-Branding Assignment example:
- Words that describe me:
    - Creative, Bold, Giving
    - Giving, Passionate, Leader
    - Bold, Driven, Gritty
    - Aggressive, Brave, Creative
    - Strong, Giving, Leader
    - Passionate, Bold, Driven
    - Resilient, Gritty, Giving
        - I would have to agree with the words that others have used to describe me. I know some of my core strengths are being a leader, creative, and I love to give. I can be aggressive from time to time, but I would hope others would not be too taken aback by my aggressive traits.
- Mantra/Tagline:
    - Empowered Encourager
    - Logo:

Words that describe me:
1.
2.
3.
4.
5.
6.
7.

Reflection:

Mantra/Slogan:

Logo:

Now that we have anchored you in with your personal brand, I want you to keep that brand locked in your core. I am the blue ladybug, and you will see her everywhere. She is the magic, and I remember that every business I build comes from her. I honor her power and all she stands for. Your identity is within, and when you are secure in self, there will be no stopping what you can create and the impact you will have. You will indeed go from startup to success.

Let us now turn our attention to building the business brand. "It's all in a name." Have you ever heard that saying before? Well, it is often true. In my welfare to wealth story, found in the back of book, I tell you about my business and how I had to have that glorious name *Start To Finish Files*—just like Ray Kroc had to have *McDonald's*. For me, STFF is exactly who I am; I finish what I start.

When you are creating your brand name, you need to be cautious of a few things. First, does someone else already have that name, and are they doing business under that name? You will need to find that out right away. But how do you even come up with a name in the first place? I would encourage you to go to a quiet place, a place that works with your highest element—water, fire, air, or earth. Sit in that quiet place and allow whatever to come to you regarding your business and name. Write down everything that comes. Don't throw anything away at first. Then go back through your list and examine what you have. But don't be too harsh on yourself. Don't judge too much. Just remember a few golden rules.

Have you ever seen the name of a business and thought, *Huh? How do you pronounce that? What does that mean?* You don't want a name that is too confusing, hard to spell, or hard to pronounce. It should not have any underlying message that only you know. It needs to be fresh and timeless because you will want it to be with you the entire time you are in business. Developing a solid brand name is very important. There is power in a name, so choose wisely. I have provided space for you to work on your name. Remember, just let everything come to you, without self-censoring.

Name Creation:

There are steps to building your brand. You will certainly need a logo. Many times, the logo is all we see. Take, for example, Starbucks. If you look at most of their products, their name is not on it, just their logo. The same is true with their storefront and store signs. Their logo has gained enough awareness that we know the little funny-looking mermaid lady in a circle is Starbucks. We don't quite know why that is their logo and what it has to do with coffee, but we recognize it, nonetheless. It is unique, and it has been undoubtedly instrumental to the success of the brand. Your logo could start off with your name on it, as Starbucks' did, but any good logo will eventually hold ground with no name needed. That is called brand awareness. The evolution of the Starbucks logo went from having the name on the logo, as well as the language coffee, tea, and spices, and then it changed to just coffee. Then, finally, nothing. No name, no product. Just that funny-looking mermaid.

To go along with your logo, you will want to create a tagline, also known as a slogan. One of the more well-known taglines is Nike's *"Just Do It."* This tagline has been around since the late 1980s. Talk about power in a slogan! Let's now have a little fun. Below are some well-known taglines. Take a moment to read them over and see if you can figure out the company they belong to.

Kid Tested. Mother Approved.
Life's Good
Trusted Everywhere
Maybe She's Born With It
We Try Harder
Keep Walking
Gather 'Round the Good Stuff
Makes Mouths Happy
Something Special in the Air
It's Not Just a Job, It's an Adventure!

How do you think you did? The answers are in the back of the book. Don't cheat and look if you didn't try. But if you did try, look now to see how you did. You might surprise yourself. That is how the programming of marketing works. The essence of your brand message is found in the tagline, and that is why it must be short, simple, clear, and, most of all, memorable. It may be difficult to do, but I am sure you can do it. For my business STFF, my tagline is *"The Better Solution."* I can promise you that I am always looking for better solutions. Not only do I look for them, but I provide them. My tagline is living, and yours should as well. In just a few moments, I am going to share with you my personal tagline and ask you to create one for yourself.

Once you develop your logo and your tagline, you will need to put those suckers on everything possible. You should have it on letterheads, envelopes, business cards, flyers, promotional pens, note pads, T-shirts, all packaging...the list goes on and on. Then make sure all your clients receive something from you with your logo on it. My STFF logo was on everything—from the fax order form to the packaging label to the Post-it inside on top of the file to the bright yellow invoice. I even had T-shirts made that my staff and I wore, and I would give them to my clients when I came around and visited them.

Slogan and Hashtag Development

Now you are going to give it a try. Spend a little time thinking about what your business slogan will be and also draft what you would like to see for your logo. Have fun and just play around. Imagine and give way to the spirit of creativity.

Logo Design (space to sketch)

I am big on branding. Part of your brand is also your appearance. So, make sure you are always put together well. Use your branding colors in your appearance—from what you wear to your accessories. You are using deep psychology when you do so. In the previous chapter, I shared with you that everything about you communicates—from the way you dress to how you smell to what comes out of your mouth to how you listen. This is why it is important to take good care of yourself. Remember, at the core, you are the brand.

There are many things that contribute to your brand and the awareness your brand attracts. Today, I am known for my shoes: high heels. It is part of my brand. I am also known for snapping my fingers—ergo, Snap Queen! That, too, is a part of my brand. Most of all I am know to for an innate ability to inspire and empower. I deliver on my promises and I keep my word. Make sure you take the time to develop your brand and remember to always deliver on your brand promise. Rules were meant to be broken, but promises were not. Keep your word and keep your promise.

"Stop selling. Start helping."

—Zig Ziglar, author and motivational speaker

When we look at marketing, the basic principle that arises is commonly known as the 4 Ps: *Product, Price, Promotion, and Place*. The model that is a better fit for startup to success, however, is the **S.A.V.E** model: *Solution (Product), Access (place), Value (price), and Education (promotion)*. From this point forward, I want you to understand that your product or service is the solution. As I shared just a few paragraphs prior, my slogan for STFF for many years has been "*The Better Solution.*" This saying is also one of my personal mantras. There is always a better solution. Period. Do not get all caught up in the features of your product or service; instead, get caught up in solving the problem for your customer or client. You are there to meet their needs—remember that. How easily accessible your business is to your target market is so important. Remember in the previous chapter when I stated that one of the problems consumers face is lack of access? I gave the example of Macy's and online shopping. You need to be aware of how quickly your target market can access your business not only for the product and or services you provide, but also for the customer support. The access approach looks at how the customer first hears about your business to when they make their first purchase. I promise you that customers and clients care very much about how receptive you are to their feedback, and how available you are to support them.

Value, value, value. It is always about value and so very little about price. People pay for value. Time and time again, studies show that if people see value—even perceived value—they will normally pay whatever you are asking. You must be diligent in showcasing your business value. Your purple cow must be on full display at all times because your value sets your price.

Education brings it home with our **S.A.V.E** model. As an educator, I love this new approach. Provide your customer or client with the most up-to-date information possible regarding your product or services. Make sure what you share with them is relevant. Have case studies and testimonials ready to share. Be able to show how your solution worked for others in the past. Case studies often show the benefits of using certain methods that are in alignment with your product or services. People are looking for proof. One of the things I share with my students on the first day of class is a book of my life's work. It shows all the different ads I ran, as well as my different marketing materials. I show the original purchase agreement between Dan and me. I show all my businesses over a period of time. I also include several testimonials. Why do I share this book with them? Because it is proof of my work. It is evidence. I am not just talking the talk; I am walking the walk, and, in their hands, they see my footprints. I am an educator. As an empowered entrepreneur, you, too, are an educator. Educators come with proof.

The marketing concept is also very important to understand. There are three components to the marketing concept: customer orientation, service orientation, and profit orientation. The **customer orientation** is all about finding out what the customers want and like, and then providing it to them. The ability to find out what the customer wants has increasingly become easier. I can almost guarantee that you have some type of rewards card. Whether it is from a grocery store, drugstore, or you simply put your number into a system to collect points, we all have some type of rewards card. Well, these lovely rewards cards are tracking our every purchase. The data that is collected from the use of the reward card gives a company valuable information. It now knows what we like, how often we use products, and so on. The company will now send you coupons for a selected set of items they know you are going to buy. Brilliant!

Customer orientation is also done by conducting surveys. Companies use surveys all the time to not only provide customers with what they want, but also to improve service. **Service orientation** is making sure everyone in the organization is committed to customer satisfaction. I started off this chapter by telling you how *marketing* is a magic show, and that the greatest marketing tool you have is word of mouth—WOM. Service orientation is your key driver for WOM. You need everyone show-ready at all times. I am very customer service focused. It is truly a part of my purple cow, my value proposition. I stand out when it comes to customer satisfaction. Because of my servant's mentality, I have been able to take little and make it much. I have been able to grow in locations, clients, and students, all because I know how important it is to provide excellent customer service. My clients and students, in turn, spread the word about me, and I grow again. Focusing on both customer orientation and service orientation is mission-critical to the success of your business, and it is the only way to be a leader in entrepreneurship in the new millennium.

Profit orientation focuses on the goods and services that will earn the most profit. This was the McDonalds' strategy when they first began. The McDonald brothers realized that what was selling and making the most profit were burgers, fries, and a drink. They eliminated everything else and focused just on that. It worked, and today, McDonald's is a billion-dollar business. This is just one example of how to use a profit orientation. The key is to focus on what is selling and earning the most profit. Those are the items you want to push.

Many times, people try to do too much. In the United States, we are always about overstuffing our faces. Fill that plate right up with as much as you can. As if you will starve if you only eat a small portion! That is so far from the truth, it is not even funny. Many times, if your plate is too full, you end up wasting the food—or even worse, stuffing yourself until you can hardly breathe and wonder why you keep gaining weight. Startup to success is all about being lean. Keep that in mind as you look at your product and/or services. Do you really need all of them? Are they all making you money? Get rid of something and see how that works. You can always bring it back if you need to. But you cannot get back the lost time and money you spend on trying to sell something that no one wants to buy.

"If you form a strategy without research, your brand will barely float—and at the speed industries move at today, brands sink fast."

—Ryan Holmes, entrepreneur

The marketing strategy process starts with the company vision. The vision of the company addresses the question, "Where is the company going?" It addresses future goals and milestones yet to be accomplished. The mission of the company addresses the following questions: Why does the business exist? What do we do? How do we do it? And for whom do we do it? Both the vision and mission provide direction for the company. Objectives are then set in place, which provides us with the steps on how we are going to get where. We say, "We desire to be…" followed by the steps we must take in order to fulfill our mission. For many years, marketing objectives have been known by an acronym called SMART: **S**pecific, **M**easurable, **A**chievable, **R**ealistic, and

Time-based. But it is a new millennium, and we need to be SMARTER, so I have added two more objectives: **E**xecutable and **R**elevant.

At one point in my life, I weighed over 300 pounds. My vision was to be a normal body weight and, above all, healthy. That is where I was going. My mission was to embody a healthy lifestyle in pursuit of my vision. I tried to lose weight many times being SMART, but then I finally became SMARTER. I want you to be a SMARTER entrepreneur, as well. I realized the objectives and critical steps I had to take to achieve my mission and, ultimately, the vision was every day. I needed to do a series of things that cultivated my new chosen lifestyle. I had to prep my food and eat the prepped food. I had to increase my water intake. I had to go to the gym. I had to do all of those steps consistently in order to achieve the results I desired. After a little over a year of discipline, staying focused on my vision, being true to my mission, and following the objectives I had laid out, I achieved one of my health goals of losing over 100 pounds. This is how the marketing strategy works. This is how many things in life work—systems, strategy, and discipline.

I want you now to take some time to think about your vision, mission, and objectives. I would even encourage you to do a little searching on the internet and read some of the top Fortune 500 companies' vision and mission statements. Then go check some small business websites and see what they have as theirs. Do the companies embody their vision and mission statements? Do you see them achieving goals, and are their objectives working? After you have done this mini-research, I want you to come back to this book and write out your vision and mission statement. I also want you to include some values and goals. Then I want you to write out your objectives. What steps do you need to take in order to reach your vision and fulfill your mission? Use the space provided to develop those steps.

Vision, Mission, and Value Development with SMARTER Business Goal Setting:

_____

_____

Now, how do you begin to do market research? Market research is the gathering and interpretation of data in a specific industry. It also includes answers to a series of questions and, more importantly, the development of your target market. There are two types of data that exist for market research: primary data and secondary data. Primary data is data you develop. You gather the information from doing research, test markets, surveys, focus groups, and so on. Secondary data is data that already exists. The research has been done for you and the information is published and available for use. There can be a cost associated with some secondary data, but overall, there is an incredible amount of solid secondary data that is available for free. As with any data, please be sure you check your sources. Make sure the sources are legitimate and reputable. Some of the information that you should be able to find out directly from secondary data is:

- The total size of your industry
- Trends in the industry—is it growing or shrinking?
- The total size of your target market and what share is realistic for you to obtain
- Trends in the target market—is it growing or shrinking? How are customer needs or preferences changing?

Below are a few additional questions that you should be able to answer from your research.

- Who are your customers?
- What do they buy now?
- Why do they buy?
- When do they buy?
- What will make them buy from you?

Who are your customers? This is one of the most important questions to answer. This is also known as your *target market.* I am always reminding my students and clients that they cannot serve everyone, nor do they really want to. Even though I do all I can to drill this into their heads, I always receive in my students' business briefs a very large target market. Then I remind them once again that they must bring in that market and be more focused. The market is broken down into segments. There are several different segments, but according to Active Marketing, an online branding and marketing research company, the list below contains the most common. Remember, you will not choose all of them. You will, however, select some.

- "***Psychographic:*** *Grouping your customers into cultural clusters, social status, lifestyle, and personality type.*
- ***Decision Makers:*** *Grouping your customers based on who decides to purchase your product within the company structure.*
- ***Behavioral:*** *Grouping customers by product usage. For example; light, medium, or heavy users. This stage also factors in brand loyalty and the type of user.*
- ***Geographic:*** *Grouping customers by a specific area, such regions of the country or state and urban or rural.*
- ***Distribution:*** *Grouping customers based on where they go to purchase your product, such as online, store, or through a catalog.*
- ***Demographic:*** *Grouping customers by age, income level, gender, family size, religion, race, nationality, language, etc.*"[24]

The marketing plan contains the competitors analysis. You will need to ensure you do research and find out who your competitors are. You will have competitors, so don't get it in your head that you will not. I had competitors. Even though they were not direct competitors because they were medical record copy services and I was a social security disability records copy service, they were competitors, nevertheless.

In the journey from startup to success, we collaborate more than we compete. Keep that in mind when you are researching your competition. Could they end up being someone you work directly with to grow and build the business? It took some time before I had a direct competitor. His name was Tony. He showed up on the scene, and I promise you, he pissed me off by arriving. I can clearly remember seeing his business card at one of the federal hearing offices I served. I took that business card, tore it apart, and threw in the garbage. I thought to myself, *Who the hell does this guy think he? Trying to come in and take a slice of my pie? Not today, buddy, not today and not ever!* Fast forward to today: Tony sends me checks on a regular basis. The scanning equipment I have today is from Tony. Tony had one thing going for him—okay, two things. First, Tony was Italian like me, and second, Tony was scanning while I was still copying records. He was ahead of the curve, and I needed to be there with him. We joined forces and created an alliance and have been the best of competitors ever since. Collaboration.... Italiano style.

Now we need to bring all our pieces together and put them into a marketing plan. I have provided a simple marketing plan below, which I suggest you use to do some developing of your own. The following information is from the SBA and is the most common marketing template information in the new millennium.

"**Target market:** *Describe your audience in detail. Look at the market's size, demographics, unique traits, and trends that relate to demand for your business.*

_____
_____
_____
_____
_____
_____
_____
_____
_____

Competitive advantage: *Describe what gives your product or service an advantage over the competition. It might be a better product, a lower price, or an excellent customer experience. Sometimes, an environmentally friendly certification or 'made in the USA' on your label can be an important factor for customers.*

_____
_____
_____
_____
_____
_____
_____
_____

Sales plan: *Describe how you'll literally sell your service or product to your customers. List the sales methods you'll use, like retail, wholesale, or your own online store. Explain each step your customer takes once they decide to buy.*

_____
_____
_____
_____
_____
_____
_____
_____

Marketing and sales goals: *Describe your marketing and sales goals for the next year. Common marketing and sales goals are to increase email subscribers, grow market share, or increase sales by a certain percent.*

_____
_____
_____
_____
_____
_____
_____
_____
_____

Marketing action plan: *Describe how you'll achieve your marketing and sales goals. List marketing channels you'll use, like online advertising, radio ads, or billboards. Explain your pricing strategy and how you'll use promotions. Talk about the customer support that happens after the sale. The federal government regulates advertising and labeling for a number of consumer products, so make sure your advertising is legally compliant.*

_____
_____
_____
_____
_____
_____
_____
_____

Budget*: Include a complete breakdown of the costs of your marketing plan. Try to be as accurate as possible. You'll want to keep tracking your costs once you put your plan into action."*[14]

_____
_____
_____
_____
_____
_____
_____
_____
_____

Marketing is a large topic and contains vast amounts of information. I could write an entire book on it—and just may one day—but for now, here is where I leave you with marketing. It is critical to your business. It would be wise to take advantage of experts that are available to you and are worth paying for. You will not want to rush through marketing research or the planning of it. You need to take your time. Marketing will need to be managed, just like many other things in your business. Be sure to reflect. Make changes and adjustments when needed. Logos and slogan designs are so great for marketing because once you have them, there will be few changes needed. For all other aspects of marketing, there will need to be adjustments made as you move forward in the future. When you do, you will go from startup to success.

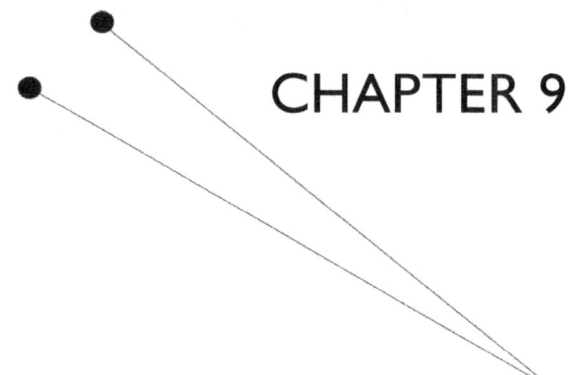

CHAPTER 9

Networking

"Networking is an investment in your business. It takes time and when done correctly can yield great results for years to come."

—Diane Helbig

Networking is going to be another major piece to your infrastructure. A cornerstone, if you will. You will need to ensure you know how to effectively communicate in order to network. In Chapter 7, I addressed communication and gave you some valuable tips that you could use. I suggest you go back and read those over again. Networking is where your flamingo is going to shine, but you will need to ensure that the lion has some control, or the flamingo could talk too much. Be sure to use them together in a beautiful dance of charm and confidence. Networking takes time and effort. But as the opening quote states, it will *yield great results for years to come.*

Let's define what networking is for this meaning of this chapter. According to the Oxford dictionary, networking is defined as "*interacting with others to exchange information and develop professional or social contacts...it's so important to network when starting a new business."* What I love is that even the dictionary states how important it is for startups to network. It is because of my network and the quality of work that I do that I was able to grow my core business the way I did. And today, as I am building my greatest empire yet, it is even more relevant and helps fuel my growth. This directly affects the impact I have, and this is what I am after. I am after impact. There are over 7 billion people on the planet, each one holding a key. Many of them have a key you need. It is important to find them and obtain the key. It is the only key that unlocks the door that you were called to walk through. Far too often, we take for granted how important people are, especially as we become even more dependent on technology. But as you will see when I address the power of human capital, we are nothing without the people.

So, how do you network? Where do you even start? Social media is the first place. I am sure you have some type of social media account. You don't need them all, but there certainly is one major player in the business world that is used all the time for networking. Do you know which one it is? Did you think it was Facebook? Well, it is not. It's LinkedIn, and you need to have an account. It is 100 percent business and holds a lot of value. LinkedIn, I will attest, was not always the best when it first started, and it was very corporate driven. However, that has changed over the years. I am now going to share with you some statistics.

According to an article written by Paige Cooper entitled "20 LinkedIn Statistics That Matter to Marketers in 2020," the LinkedIn user stats are as follows:

1. "LinkedIn has 675 million monthly users
2. 57% of LinkedIn users are men, and 43% are women
3. 27% of Americans use LinkedIn
4. 51% of Americans with a college education use LinkedIn
5. 70% of LinkedIn's users are outside the U.S.
6. 61% of LinkedIn's users are between 25 and 34 years old

7. 57% of LinkedIn's traffic is mobile

8. LinkedIn has 15x more content impressions than job postings

9. Engagement has increased 50%, year over year

10. Users are 60% more likely to engage with a coworker than another connection

11. 30% of a company's engagement on LinkedIn comes from employees

12. Employees are 14x more likely to share content from their employers than other types of content on LinkedIn.

13. 4 out of 5 people on LinkedIn "drive business decisions"

14. An ad on LinkedIn can reach 12% of the world's population

15. 30 million companies are on LinkedIn

16. 94% of B2B marketers use LinkedIn for content marketing

17. 89% of B2B marketers use LinkedIn for lead generation

18. 59% of sales professionals count on social platforms to sell

19. Sponsored InMail has a 52% open rate, on average

20. Cost per lead on LinkedIn is 28% lower than on Google AdWords"[25]

That is one powerful hub, don't you think? I suggest you take time to build up your LinkedIn profile. If you don't have one, I need you to stop reading right now and go create an account. I am on there, and you can connect with me. I am building my LinkedIn and, truth be told, I could use it more than what I do, but I certainly use it more now than I did when it first came out. I have a nice network of businesses, and I showcase my work on the platform. I've had many calls and Zoom meetings with contacts from my LinkedIn network, and they have benefited me greatly.

Facebook is also a powerful tool you can use to build your network. Now, I am not going to assume, but unless you are completely anti-social media, I imagine you probably have a Facebook account. You will want to create one if you don't. Facebook started off as a way for friends and family to stay connected across the globe but quickly evolved into the building of businesses as well. There is much to learn about how to effectively use Facebook with regards to marketing, and I suggest you take a class or two to learn more. If you have a Facebook account, then you have a network already. Leverage that network by posting about your startup and ask your family and friends to share your post. Each time they share it, your post touches another cluster of people.

Here are some statistics for Facebook:

"Facebook has 2.60 billion monthly active users (Facebook, 2020). If that number doesn't blow you away, it also has 1.73 billion users that are visiting the social networking site on a daily basis.

When it comes to social media, Facebook remains the undefeated champion. Based on the statistics, Facebook is the leading social platform, reaching 60.6 percent of internet users (Facebook, 2018).

In the first quarter of 2020, the company brought in $17.44 billion in ad revenue (Facebook, 2020). That puts its average revenue per user at $6.95. Not only does this make up nearly all (98.3 percent) of its $17.737 billion revenue for the entire quarter, it's also a 17 percent year-over-year increase from the first quarter of 2019.

Facebook has more than 80 million small businesses around the world using Facebook Pages (Facebook, 2018). Your Facebook Page is a place where you can share your business name, address, contact details, and a description about the products or services that your business offers. It gives you the possibility to increase the online presence of your business. The reason why so many people are using Facebook Pages for their business, is because of the benefits linked to having one. Through Facebook, businesses can reach one of the world's largest communities

Seven out of ten (69%) adults in the U.S. claim that they use Facebook (Pew Research Center, 2019). What's interesting to note is that the share of U.S. adults using social media, including Facebook, is mostly unchanged since 2018. This is despite a series of controversies over privacy, fake news, and censorship on social media, especially Facebook.

Contrary to popular belief, Facebook still remains the dominant social media platform for young adults. 65 percent of Facebook users are under the age of 35 (Statista, 2019), which means that they fall under the age demographic of Millennials and Generation Z. This Facebook statistic also shows us that for the most part, young adults prefer to use similar social media platforms to interact with others their age.

One of the reasons why Facebook has become such a huge social network worldwide is due to its mobile accessibility. Unrestricted access through multiple mobile apps, as well as its mobile website has given Facebook an edge over competitors that didn't think of mobile first. 96 percent of active Facebook users accessed the social media platform via mobile devices, which includes tablets or smartphones (DataReportal, 2019). That means that only 4 percent of Facebook active users logged in on desktop devices to use the social

When it comes to time spent on Facebook, users spend an average of 58.5 minutes on the social media platform each day (Recode, 2018). So, as well as being the most popular social media platform, Facebook users are also visiting the site multiple times per day. Whether it's scrolling down your newsfeed while waiting in line for your groceries, on the train to work, or that last scroll before you go to sleep—no one can disagree that Facebook plays a significant role in our daily lives.

Being the biggest social media site out there, Facebook gets its fair share of attention from marketers as well. For instance, in the U.S., 86 percent of marketers are using Facebook for advertising (Emarketer, 2018). Regardless of the size of your business, Facebook is a great place to start your social media marketing efforts.

Facebook is connecting people to brands and products. In fact, 78 percent of American consumers have discovered retail products to buy via Facebook (Kleiner Perkins, 2018). The survey suggests that more than half of the people have used Facebook to actively look for products, with the majority of them discovering new products on Facebook's News Feed, Pages, and Groups." [26]

As you can see, Facebook is extremely powerful, and you will want to leverage that power. I have a Facebook account, a few pages, and one core group I manage. I can attest to it being hard to manage it all. I have a Professor Palumbo Facebook page. This was the first page I created. I did this so my students could stay connected with me. I was not public like I am now, so I didn't accept friend requests from students, so I needed a place for them to be able to stay connected with me. When I wrote my first book, *Entrepreneurship Empowered*, I created another page for that book. Then I wrote my fourth book, *Empowered Life*, and I have a women's empowerment group I created. The group is private and just for women. It is Empowered Life: Healing the Feminine Spirit, A New Birth to Sisterhood. I have a lovely group of over 150 women and growing. A large chunk of my work is dedicated to helping women heal. I care deeply for men, too, and I hold great space for their healing as well.

However, I am a woman, and I know how broken the sisterhood is, and how it is deeply tied to motherhood issues. We hear a lot about fatherhood issues, but we don't hear enough about the toxic mother. But I expose the elephant in the room. I eat that sucker one bite at a time. This women's empowerment group is doing just that. I leverage this network of women by serving them because, in networking, it is not about taking but rather giving. Then, naturally, you will receive. I host free events with my ladies on a regular basis. I'm big on challenges, and so each month I do some type of challenge. I serve them the best I can by sharing my life story. More so, I share how, no matter what comes at you in this life, you can overcome any obstacle. I give to them, and in return, they build my network by telling other women about the group and inviting them to the events I hold. I am building exposure and a networking that will grow. I am generous with myself and my offerings. It is not about the harvest you reap today but the seeds you plant.

"The currency of real networking is not greed but generosity."

—Keith Ferrazzi, author

One final social media networking site to address is Instagram. I love the gram so much. This has to be one of my favorite networking sites. I have my largest following there, and it, too, is growing. I am a photographer and very creative, so the gram allows me to go wild. This was the first place I went public. I went public in June of 2018. At that time, I had about 200 followers. I started working with a branding and social media expert: Nicky Saunders, CEO of Beast Mode Digital. She works with some major players, one of which is Dr. Eric Thomas, also known as "ET, The Hip Hop Preacher." He is one of the top motivational speakers in the world. Working with Nicky was nothing short of amazing. You may contact her at nicky@beastmode-digital.com for more information. She immediately gave me tools and so much value. I mean, her purple cow was incredible! With her advice and recommendations—and my hard work—my following began to grow and continues to grow daily. In my first month of being public, I grew 100 percent. Each month after, the growth continued to be very high. How do I do that, you ask? I use hashtags.

Now, the hashtag game is an interesting one. It worked for a really long time, then Instagram changed its algorithms, and it lost its pull. I am still growing, but not at the same rate as I was. All the growth I saw in the beginning was very organic. I do leverage what I have grown, and I use ads to promote my books and events. They work, but they take time to master. I'm still learning how to master them. What I have done is built a great brand awareness and network to pull from. I'm able to leverage my network from Instagram to build attendance for my events, but more so people see what I am doing and then they contact me to learn more about how I can come and help them. I use the story feature daily, and I post all kinds of different things—from random life stuff to a new book release to a workshop I'm hosting to an event that I will be speaking at. This is a showcase of my work and my life. This is what draws others in so that I may serve them and have a greater impact. What is so great is on both Facebook and Instagram, others share about me. This expands my network and helps me grow it. This is how you go from startup to success!

Social media is not the only place to do your networking. There are many other opportunities and events at your disposal. You will find a host of networking events going on all the time. If you have never been to a networking event, I highly recommend you go to one. There are in-person events, as well as virtual ones. Have your business cards ready to go and, more importantly, make sure to pick up other people's cards and follow up with them. When building your network, you want to think about your target market and then build a circle around them. Start by identifying who they are. I had you do that in the last chapter. Once you've accomplished that, I need you to identify where they might be, who might work with them, who might serve them. Here is an example: a large target for me is the underserved. I am here for them. So, I need to build my network with social services that care for the underserved. Then, I'm able to work with my target market and be paid for the work I do. My network needs to be built with nonprofits, county department of health and welfare, and the like. That means I need to be at networking events where underserved people will be attending. You understand? I'm making connections outside of my direct target. The same is true for you.

I'm going to give you some space to write out this next activity: I want you to make a list of the important contacts in your network. These will be individuals who may provide information to you, advice, inspiration, encouragement, and the like. When you write them down, you can note what it is that you get from each person. What value does the exchange you have with them bring to your life? Then, I want you to note next to their name who introduced you to them. How was it that you met? If you introduced yourself to them, then just put "me." In networking, there are brokers, and if you are familiar with what brokers do, they connect. In real estate, they connect buyers to sellers. My dear friend Henry Einstein, who wrote the foreword for this book, is a real estate broker and a powerful connector. This young man is a business genius, and he is able to not only connect buyers to sellers, but his ability to network is out of this world. Today, he has a strong network of individuals who have influence, affiliations, wealth, and power. For the purpose of this activity, the person who connected you with your contact is the broker. You are going to need to find out who your brokers are. If you see "me" appear too many times, you know that you have an inbred network.

In an article titled "How to Build Your Network," which was featured in the *Harvard Business Review*, Brian Uzzi and Shannon Dunlap write:

"According to our studies, if you've introduced yourself to your key contacts more than 65% of the time, then you're probably building your network using the self-similarity principle and your network may be too inbred. The self-similarity principle states that, when you make network contacts, you tend to choose people who resemble you in terms of experience, training, worldview, and so on. We have found that executives, in particular, disproportionately use the self-similarity principle to build their networks. Obviously, it is easier to trust someone who views the world through the same lens you do; you expect that person to act as you would in ambiguous

situations. What's more, working with people who share your background is often very efficient: You both recognize concepts that allow you to transfer information quickly, and you are less likely to challenge one another's ideas. Finally, like-minded people will usually affirm your point of view and, as a result, gratify your ego. Too much similarity restricts your access to discrepant information, which is crucial to both creativity and problem solving. If all your contacts think the way you do, who will question your reasoning or push you to expand your horizon? And because, over time, people tend to introduce their contacts to one another so that everyone becomes friends, the similarity of thought and skill reverberates, creating what we call an echo chamber."[27]

Now, if you find that you have another name appearing, this person is known as your super connector, and this person is definitely someone you want to keep on your team. Make them the first person you share information to, as they will disburse it with their network. The other names that appear on your list are your brokers, and you want to make sure you leverage them as well. Then, you will need to expand your reach beyond these brokers and see if you can build some more. Attending mixers, whether it be online or in person, will benefit you as you build your network. I highly recommend you jump into any organizations that cater to startups. I am located in Sacramento, and here we have what's called "StartupSac," and every Wednesday they host a free virtual event called 1 Million Cups. This is a networking event where startups get to pitch. However, they are pitching for feedback, not for an actual ask like you would in a pitch-off competition. You could present at the 1 Million Cups, and they are all over the nation. Also, by just attending, you are being exposed to others in the field of startup. You must use your resources and build your network. When you do, you will go from startup to success.

Let's take a moment to do some networking drafting. I want you to think about all I have given you so far, from the social media networking to your target market to finding out who your brokers and who your super connectors are. I want you to write what comes to you, and I want you to make sure you do your list. Then, I want you to check out 1 Million Cups. Find out when the next one is in your area and attend. Then I want you do a search for other networking events. For the events, I want you to attend a couple. Remember to have your business cards ready. Do not let the flamingo run wild. Control it with the lion and shine like the star you are. Take time now to draft and research.

Networking Activity:

_____
_____
_____
_____
_____
_____
_____
_____
_____
_____
_____
_____
_____
_____
_____
_____
_____
_____
_____
_____

Some final notes on networking, I want you to understand you are building trust. Therefore, you must be a trustworthy person and do right by people. Bad business, no matter how long the run, will always end in destruction. Do yourself a favor and do right by people. Make sure you are a person of your word. If you say you will do something, then do it. If you make a contact at an event and you tell them you will be contacting them, you should honor your word. You never know when you are being linked to a broker who could link you to your next big break.

I need you to make networking a priority and understand it requires you to invest your time. You cannot build your business alone. Even if you are going to be a sole proprietor, you are still an empowered entrepreneur, which means you understand that you need people on your team and you need to make finding and connecting with them a priority. I want your efforts in networking to be sincere. I want you to be a person who is confident in who they are and the purpose they have to offer this world. I want you to be heart centered and understand that you have power in the position of humility. This will be instrumental to your success.

Being humble and heart centered is tied into emotional intelligence. You are going to need emotional intelligence and understand the emotions of others. I tell my students and clients all the time, learn as much as you can about trauma. Why? Because everyone has it. Primary, secondary, or both, no one gets out of this life without trauma. And if you do not think you have trauma, well, you have been going through the pandemic of 2020, also known as COVID-19. So you have trauma from that event and all that came with it. We, as a world, will be healing from COVID-19 for a long time. This is why I need you to learn about trauma and why people do what they do. We are energy in motion. We are e-motion. Becoming more emotionally intelligent will not only help you personally, but you will be a better leader, your network will be built with strong players—like my dear friend Henry—and your business will benefit. You will go from startup to success.

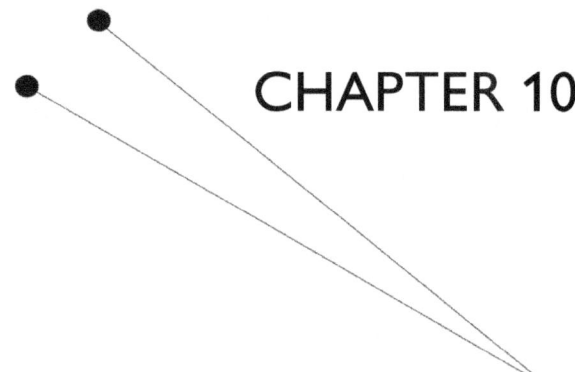

CHAPTER 10

The Power of Human Capital

"In business, the most important lesson I have learned is that there is one currency that always plays the key role in forming value, and that is human capital—the knowledge, skills and experiences of people."

—Lowell Milken, international businessman and philanthropist

You are in the human economy. It has always been here. You see, no matter which economy we have been in, from agriculture to technology, it has taken the human to produce the work. Yes, even with technology. We need the human to create the technology, and then, when it breaks down, we need the human to come and fix it. Technology will never overtake the human economy because the human has a set of skills that technology will never have. We are unique. We have a soul and emotions. That is something technology will never have. At least I hope not. That is where things could really go wrong. It is the emotions that cause us to do many of the things we do. This is why emotional intelligence is absolutely necessary and why you have seen it addressed many times in this book. I need you to understand you are to benefit, uplift, encourage, and empower the human economy, starting with yourself. The way out is within. The more you develop yourself, the better you will be able to serve others. Without your human capital, you really do not have a business. I could not have grown my business the way I did without my human capital. The work you are doing as an empowered entrepreneur will require you to have solid human capital.

According to Investopedia, *"human capital is an intangible asset or quality not listed on a company's balance sheet. It can be classified as the economic value of a worker's experience and skills. This includes assets like education, training, intelligence, skills, health, and other things employers' value such as loyalty and punctuality. The concept of human capital recognizes that not all labor is equal. But employers can improve the quality of that capital by investing in employees—the education, experience, and abilities of employees all have economic value for employers and for the economy as a whole. Human capital is important because it is perceived to increase productivity and thus profitability. So, the more a company invests in its employees (i.e., in their education and training), the more productive and profitable it could be."*[28]

Your human capital is managed by your human resources (HR) department, which, for my business, was me, and for you it will be the same. The one thing for sure is that when you are starting up your business, you do most of the work. Handling the HR side of things is one of the roles you'll be fulfilling. I did have an accountant who took care of my employee taxes and payroll. You will want to look at making sure you have accountant on your team too. I was able to handle all that was required in regard to HR because my company wasn't that large. However, each business will differ in terms of its needs, but there will be a common theme with all businesses: there will always be a recruiting and selection process. You will need to create job descriptions prior to posting job announcements. The job description should be detailed. It's important to include certain elements in your job posting that are mission-critical to the job—like lifting, typing, software comprehension, and so on. You will need to be clear on your vision, mission, and values because you will want to attract those whose values are in alignment with yours.

You will get a string of résumés submitted. Many times, employers will get hundreds of résumés a day. Depending on the economy, that is. But overall, people are always looking for work. Finding good help is very hard, however. You will go through all the résumés submitted and narrow them down by those who fit the job description. After you have selected your three to five potential candidates, you will then move into the interview process. It is good practice to have a set of standard interview questions. This makes the interviewing process fair for all candidates. Your questions should include things that pertain to the job in which the candidate is being interviewed. You will also want to have questions that deal with conflict resolution. Behavior questions are critical, too, because they will tell you if the person will fit in with your work culture. Not everyone is fit for your culture, and that is important to understand. You will want to have some ethical dilemma-based questions. They are just as important as all the other questions. You want an ethical person working for you.

After the interview, you will move into the selection process, check references, move forward with an offer, and finally hire the right person. This is where the paperwork madness comes into play. New hire paperwork will consist of government-required forms such as the I-9 and W-4. You can go directly to IRS.gov and pull the forms you need. They have a forms section, and the IRS website is fairly user-friendly. The forms are where a person will indicate the number of deductions they will be claiming, which indicates the amount of taxes that will be taken from one's income. Also, you will need to ensure you have an Employer Identification Number (EIN). You must have that in order to have employees but not to hire contractors, which is also an option. Contractors are not employees, and they require a scope of work, but you may want to consider taking on contractors versus employees. You will need to do further research on contractors and see if it works for you or not.

Another important piece of the new hire process is clearly laying out how compensation works (i.e., how and when they will be paid). Most payments are now done by direct deposit. You may want to consider this as a way of paying your staff. In order to make direct deposits, you will not only need to have employees fill out a form, but you will need their banking information as well. The form they fill out will allow you to have access to their account for the sole purpose of depositing funds. A lot of employers will also give employees a schedule showing exactly when payday occurs. This helps employees manage their money and the bills they have to pay.

You will also need to think about benefits. There are required benefits, no matter the size of your business. According to the SBA, those benefits are:

- *"Social Security taxes: Employers must pay Social Security taxes at the same rate as their employees*
- *Workers' Compensation: Required through a commercial carrier, self-insured basis, or state Workers' Compensation Program*
- *Disability Insurance: Disability pay is required in California, Hawaii, New Jersey, New York, Rhode Island, and Puerto Rico*
- *Leave benefits: Most leave benefits are optional outside those stipulated in the Family and Medical Leave Act (FMLA)*
- *Unemployment insurance: Varies by state, and you may need to register with your state workforce agency"*[14]

Health insurance is another benefit that employers offer. I only had part-time employees, so I did not offer health insurance. However, if you do have full-time employees, you will need to consider offering them health insurance. I highly recommend you do research not only on the Affordable Care Act, but on all the different types of health care plans available for employers. Below you will find additional bullet points of all that I have covered so far, plus a little more. The following information comes directly from Workable, a recruiting software company. They help you find, track, and hire employees.

- *"An employment contract should include:*

o   Job information (job title, department)
  o   Work schedule
  o   Length of employment
  o   Compensation and benefits
  o   Employee responsibilities
  o   Termination conditions
- Most common types of employment forms to complete are:
  o   W-4 form (or W-9 for contractors)
  o   I-9 Employment Eligibility Verification form
  o   State Tax Withholding form
  o   Direct Deposit form
  o   E-Verify system: This is not a form, but a way to verify employee eligibility in the U.S.
- Possible internal forms.
  o   Non-compete agreements
  o   Non-disclosure agreements
  o   Employee invention forms
  o   Employee handbook acknowledgement forms
  o   Drug and/or alcohol test consent agreements
  o   Job analysis forms (responsibilities, goals and performance evaluation criteria)
  o   Employee equipment inventory lists
  o   Confidentiality and security agreements
- Most common employee benefits are:
  o   Life and health insurance
  o   Mobile plan
  o   Company car
  o   Stock options
  o   Retirement plan
  o   Disability insurance
  o   Paid time off/vacation policies (including any paid holidays)

- *Sick leave*
- *Employee wellness perks (e.g., gym memberships)*
- *Tuition reimbursement*
- *Obtain employees' personal data for emergencies*
- *Emergency contacts*
- *Brief medical history*"[29]

You will need to safeguard all the information you have on your staff. You will need to have locked cabinets or even an encrypted virtual file storage. It is your job to keep your records safe.

You should also have some type of onboarding process where new employees come in to not only do paperwork but receive training. The onboarding process is a magical time for the new hire. They are now beginning to see how your organization is being managed. This will tell them a lot. If you are not well managed, they may think they've made the wrong decision to work for you. You will need to ensure that everything you provide your new hire is up to date, relevant, and that you also fully engage them in your culture. This is the time to really showcase your mission and all your company stands for. Your new hire said yes because they believe their purpose aligns with your mission. They believe they are there to help make an impact with you. Make sure you do not let them down by not having a system for your new hires. You are now going to work on creating what some of those systems look like.

Creating a New Hire Packet and Employee Handbook

I want you to indicate what will need to be in your new hire paperwork. I want you to describe how you will process the paperwork, how you plan to file it, how you will keep it organized, and so on. Then, I want you to spend some time thinking about what you will need to include in a new employee handbook. What do you believe is going to be important information that will help each of your employees? Remember, when putting your paperwork together, think about non-competition and/or intellectual property protection with any trade secrets and the like. Again, be a researcher and see what is already out there. Then, then using the space provided, write out your plan.

_____
_____
_____
_____
_____
_____
_____
_____
_____
_____
_____
_____
_____
_____
_____
_____
_____
_____
_____
_____

Creating an Onboarding Process

It always surprises me to find out how many businesses do not have an onboarding process. This is not going to be the case with your business because you are an empowered entrepreneur. If you train your employees right the first time, you don't have to train them over and over again. So, make sure to start off with a solid onboarding process. I want you to spend some time thinking about all the steps that will need to be covered in training. Don't leave anything out. No matter how skilled someone is, they will still need to know how you like the business to be run, how you like things to be done, and how your specific system works. Just spend some time thinking and draft what you believe would be a start to an onboarding process. And remember, each employee will learn and train differently. It would be wise to have them take a VARK survey to find out what their learning style is. Once you know what their most dominant learning style is, then you can teach them using that style. I do suggest you do some research about onboarding and see what you come up with. Use the space provided to write what you find.

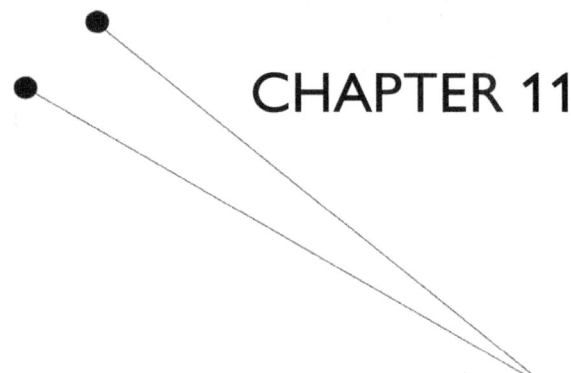

CHAPTER 11

Leadership

"The function of leadership is to produce more leaders, not more followers."

—Ralph Nader, political activist

I love the above quote because, well, I truly believe that is what makes a great leader. Not that I have more followers, but rather that I am able to build up more leaders. Many of the employees I've had throughout the years have gone on to hold leadership roles. Several of them have become business owners themselves. Today, many of my students become leaders, and, most importantly, they become stronger at leading their own lives. To me, this is one of the greatest gifts I'm able to give them.

I want you to think for a moment about some great leaders. They can be anyone from celebrities to bosses to family, even fictional characters. Think about what made them such great leaders. If they are personal leaders to you, what is it you really admired about them? Why did you see them as such great leaders? After that, I want you to think about what types of behaviors they had. What type of spirit did they carry? Then, for a moment, I want you to think about the concept of being a born leader versus being able to build a leader. In the space provided, write what comes to you.

Are leaders made, or are they born? I swear I came out of the womb saying, "*Charge, forward we go!*" For the longest time, I really felt like I was a natural-born leader and that all great leaders must have been born that way. Many of you may feel the same way. However, I will tell you that leaders can be made. As I stated above, I believe that true leaders build up more leaders. I also firmly believe that a boss will tell you what to do, but a leader will show you. A leader will get on the ground with you. I promise you that I am working right alongside you. I am leading by example.

As I have grown in my leadership ability, I have learned that leadership, like so many other things in life, is an inside job. That means you must be able to lead yourself. Are there leaders out there who are not right within? Absolutely. But in my humble opinion, I believe they will never reach the highest vibrational leadership level unless they are able to be right within. I know this doesn't seem true, especially in the world we live in (aka "the jungle"). But I can attest from my own experience that I was a great leader, but once I got my shit together and started healing within, I became a ridiculously amazing leader—my highest vibrational leadership level yet. I am building up more leaders now than ever before. I am also serving more of the masses than ever before. My territory has expanded, and my leadership role has increased. Some of you are great leaders, but I need you to become ridiculously amazing leaders. I cannot, nor do I wish, to be out in these streets alone. I need you to understand that *the way out is within*. It is your job to help free yourself so that you may serve others and provide them with the tools they need to be free. Remember, freedom comes in pieces—this is yet another piece given to you today.

Leaders commonly have a core set of qualities. Though each leader is different in their own right, they do tend to share a couple of similar traits. *Honesty and integrity* are often right at the top of the list. These qualities will tie directly in with ethics, which we will cover in just a few paragraphs. People can smell fakeness, and far too often, liars are only really lying to themselves. Eventually, the truth comes out, one way or another. In business, leaders must be honest and have integrity. If not, they will create a culture that is dishonest—a business that is dishonest. You can look at the Enron case and see that corrupt leadership only leads to corrupt business. If you haven't heard about the Enron case, I recommend you examine it. That will hold space for a very long time as an example of what not to do in business. It's one of the most highly discussed and studied ethics cases in the United States and around the world.

Confidence is also critical to leadership, especially because leadership is about inspiring others. In order to truly inspire, you must be confident in what you are offering to others. You must be able to have confidence in your people that they will do right by you, that they will take what you are giving them, and that they will run with it. Again, true leaders are building up other leaders, not followers.

Please don't confuse arrogance with confidence. Arrogant leaders are often single-minded. They believe they are superior. They may be highly intelligent, but they are usually socially inept. You know someone like that, don't you? Confident leaders don't need to offend others. They see the potential in others and have a desire to help them succeed. Confident leaders will rarely tell you how wrong you are. They will give you advice and wisdom on how to be a better person. They will never put you down for being human. Arrogant leaders, however, will ridicule you and often belittle you, even in front of your peers. So much bullying goes on in the workplace, and as a result, the employee turnover rate is extremely high. So is poor performance.

Communication style is very different in an arrogant leader than in a confident leader. An arrogant leader is always trying to one-up almost everything that is said and done. A confident leader is not going to impose his or her vision on you, but rather inspire you by showing how powerful and accomplished one is, or can be, by fulfilling the vision. Being an effective communicator is mandatory for good leadership. Effective communication not only comes from speaking, but also listening and observation. All great leaders will take the time to listen to those under their command. They will also observe, in order to hear what isn't spoken. Then they will take what they have learned and use it when they communicate their message.

Words are extremely powerful. Another main reason why I am now a ridiculously amazing leader, in addition to getting my shit together and healing within, is because I understand the power of words. I speak life and I use my words to *EMPOWER* and uplift those I serve and lead. I encourage others to do the same. "*I am…*" is by far the most powerful statement of all, because what you put after, you will ultimately be. Two other little words that are very powerful: THANK YOU! I cannot tell you how often those two words are underused. You've probably done many things in your life and not received a thank you. Well, guess what? Right now, I say THANK YOU! For what it's worth, this world will be disrespectful time and time again. I encourage you not to be disrespectful. If you are a leader, you had better know how to be respectful and have gratitude or you will stay below par and your vibrational level will eventually be no more.

Humility is a core competency of a leader. I have more power on the ground in a place of humility than I do standing above you, screaming and waving my hands around like a crazy lady—which I can do, mind you, because I am an Italian who gets loud and talks with her hands. But now I use that energy to tell jokes and entertain. With leadership, I am much more humble. Being humble and using emotional intelligence allows me to hold space for others, make sound decisions, and be more creative. A good study to look at is that of Ou, Waldman, and Peterson. It was published in the *Journal of Management* in 2015, and the article is entitled "Do Humble CEOs Matter?" This study of 105 IT companies found that greater humility in their CEOs was associated with greater leadership team integration, greater collaboration and cooperation, and greater flexibility in strategic orientation.[30]

Humble leaders are working toward the good of others and society, not themselves. Humble leaders stay hungry. They never stop learning, they are authentic in every way, they give up being right, and they give way to asking the right questions. They have a servant's heart and understand the true power of service.

Emotional intelligence is something you have seen me address several times in this book. Here it is, yes, again. I promise you, the more emotionally intelligent you become, the freer you are, the more powerful you become, and the more impact you have. Going from startup to success will demand you to be emotionally intelligent. Brilliance takes many forms—emotional intelligence is one of those forms. It allows you to have acute awareness of your own emotions and the emotions of those around you. That acute awareness is crucial for sound decision-making, which we all know is required in leadership. With regard to others, you can create strategies that keep them grounded as you deliver either good or bad news. Mental health is an epidemic in our world. The jungle is filled with the craziest animals you have ever seen. You are one of them. (Don't look at my words like that, you know I am telling the truth. You get hangry, too!)

Emotionally intelligent leaders tend to have a better grasp on mental health and are able to assess the mental state of their employees. They know if someone is suffering from depression, anxiety, grief, trauma, and the like. They are then able to serve them by providing the resources they need. Being supportive has a direct effect on the productivity of the business. The healthier the employees, the healthier the company. Emotionally intelligent leaders understand the importance of humor. Laughter is medicine for the soul, they say, and I would have to agree. I am confident you have laughed at me several times while reading this book. I promise you that I am much funnier in person. You can connect with me in person or even virtually, and I will work one-on-one with you regarding your business needs. My services come with a fee, of course, but my jokes are free.

"You can't relate to a superhero, to a superman, but you can identify with a real man who in times of crisis draws forth some extraordinary quality from within himself and triumphs but only after a struggle."

—Timothy Dalton, British actor

I remember it like it was yesterday. Dan Acland, the man I worked for and bought my business from, told me something I have never forgotten and that I share with my students and clients all the time: *"When the plane is crashing, DO NOT PANIC. Get up from the pilot's seat, walk calmly to the back of the plane, fix the plane, calmly walk to the front of the plane, have a seat in the pilot's seat, and continue to fly the plane."* A leader is not a leader if they are not able to handle crisis. You will not convince me otherwise. In the startup world, you must be able to handle crises. They are going to happen time and time again. I started off this chapter by telling you how important it is to be right within to be a highly effective leader. That power within you is what will help you in times of crisis. You will draw on that strength and you will lead your team and all those around you to safety. The following excerpt comes from an article in *Forbes*, entitled "How Training Like A Pilot Will Set You Up For Success In Crisis Management," by Robert Glazer. *"Pilots engage in some of the most rigorous training of any profession. They constantly prepare for disastrous situations and practice maneuvers that are unlikely to occur, such as landing a plane with one engine. While most of us will never face these situations, there is a core principle that pilots are taught for handling emergencies that we could all learn from: the ANC protocol. The ANC protocol stands for Aviate, Navigate and Communicate, in that order.*

- *Aviate – Maintain control of the aircraft*
- *Navigate – Know where you are and where you intend to go*
- *Communicate – Let someone know your plans and needs"*[31]

Communication comes after gaining control and figuring out what needs to be done. This takes place inside the mind and heart of a leader. Communication is not needed any time before that. It will only cause panic. Just imagine, if you will, staying with the plane example, how much panic and chaos would erupt if a pilot jumped right to communicating issues to the passengers on board. The energy alone would bring down the plane. We underestimate energy so much. It is critical for the pilot to take control, navigate, and then release information as needed. I highly recommend you research crisis tactics, and even examine the military. They deal with crisis situations all the time. The better equipped you are to handle crisis, the more successful you will be in life and in business. Whatever you do, DO NOT PANIC.

There is great power in remaining calm. I want you to remember this, not just in business, but also in your daily life. You are the leader of your life. Make sure to stay calm when emotions run high. I need you to fully activate your emotional intelligence and use every drop of it. When crises arise—and they will—I need you to take control of them. I need you to look at them with a clear mind. Being sober-minded is very important. Calm is your superpower. Let's take a closer look at that. The following are definitions from the dictionary:

- **Calm** is having the absence of strong emotions
- **Super** refers to an extraordinary ability
- **Power** is the capacity and size of your influence

So how do you stay calm under pressure? It starts with your overall character. It starts with your thought process. There is great power in positive thinking. Most great leaders who operate out of a calm demeanor have an incredible mind. They are very positive in thought and in nature. American philosopher and psychologist William James once said, *"The greatest weapon against stress is our ability to choose one thought over another."* When stressful thoughts come into your mind, you must release them. You must not give way to them because they are cancerous and will multiply like gremlins. You need to avoid them, just like you need to avoid negative people. They, too, can cause you great stress. Energy is real. It is important as a leader to be careful with your energy—what you give off and what you receive—especially during a time of crisis.

Another skill a calm leader has is that they understand how important it is to only focus on one thing at a time. Multitasking is an illusion, and though many people believe they are a master of it, they are only delaying themselves from truly being effective and efficient. They are really training themselves to be distracted. The brain can only think of one thing at a time. Multitasking often makes you speed up, but what you really need to do is slow down. When you slow down, you can be more engaged in the task at hand and churn out better work. The same goes for problem-solving. When you slow down and break the problem into smaller pieces, you can solve the issue. Leadership is an art. It seems to be dying in our world. Therefore, I need you to rise up and remember that you are an empowered entrepreneur. You are going to be the catalyst that brings life back to leadership. It all starts with you. You must train your mind to be calm. You must remember that it is one of your superpowers.

There are two leadership theories I not only teach but practice myself. *Situational leadership* is one, and *transformation leadership* is the other. **Situational leadership** has its origin from the early 1970s but still holds value today in the new millennium. It was developed by Ken Blanchard and Paul Hersey. It is a practical guide to almost any workplace situation. Can you guess the main theme behind situational leadership? The name really says it. It is based on the situation at hand. The best leadership style to use is dependent on the situation. It is also dependent on the maturity and skill level of the followers. This changes from situation to situation and from person to person.

STARTUP TO SUCCESS

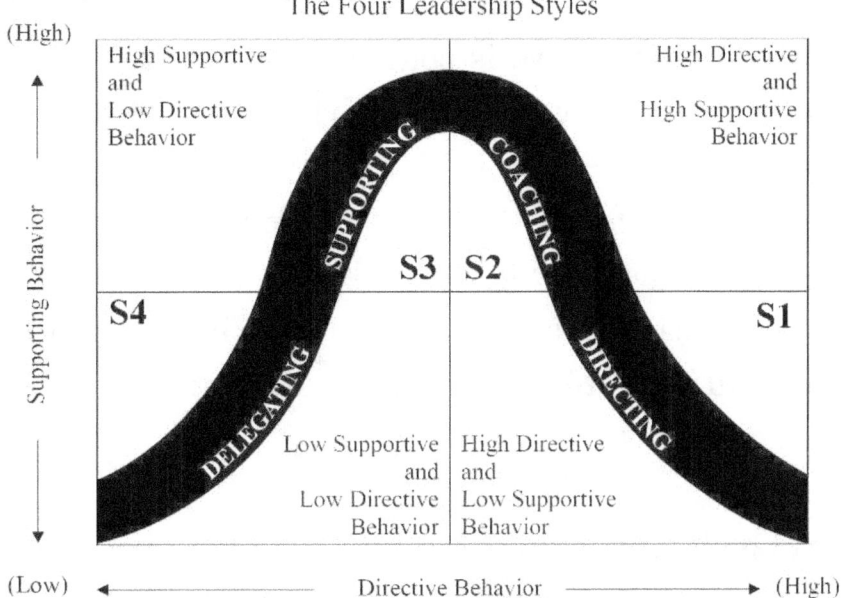

Follower Maturity	Leadership Style	Leadership Behavior	Guidance
Followers are unable to do the task and insecure.	S1 Directing	High Task & Low Relationship	Define the roles and task for each follower and then supervise them closely. Important decisions are to be made by the leader and announced to the followers.
Followers are unable to take responsibility but are willing to take on the task.	S2 Coaching	High Task & High Relationship	Define the roles and tasks of each follower, but also seek ideas and suggestions from followers. The leader coaches the followers as they develop their skills and abilities.
Followers are experienced and able to do the task but are unwilling to take on the responsibility.	S3 Supporting	Low Task & High Relationship	The leader shares decision making with the followers. A participating leader will facilitate discussions and lead the followers toward increased control over the work.
Followers are experienced in the task and confident in the ability.	S4 Delegating	Low Task & Low Relationship	While still involved in the decision, the delegating leader allows the followers to "run their own show". In fact the followers will decide when to get leader involve.

Both charts were created by Entrepreneurship Empowered based on the Situational Leadership Model by Blanchard and Hersey

There are four different leadership styles within situational leadership: style one is **directing**, style two is **coaching**, style three is **supporting**, and style four is **delegating**. View the charts to better understand. If you attend one of my classes, I will go into more detail regarding situational leadership. But for now, I would like for you to take some time to review the information on the charts and try the activity that follows.

Below is a set of situations. You are going to choose what to do, and what you choose to do will indicate what type of leadership style you used. Use the charts to help you.

Situational Leadership Styles Activity

1. You are the project manager of a six-man team. You encourage your team and notice that they work well together. However, a conflict arises between two team members regarding which idea to use in the next stage of the project. As their leader, you:

_____
_____
_____

What is your leadership style?

_____
_____
_____

2. You are the new head basketball coach. You notice that morale is low, the players are not performing at the level you know they are capable of, and they lack new skill techniques that you know will help them be more successful in the game. In a meeting, you:

_____
_____
_____

What is your leadership style?
_____
_____
_____

3. You hire a new employee who has a strong administrative skill set. After only a few weeks with the new employee, you can tell she is innovative and communicates well with clients. At first, you:
_____
_____
_____

What is your leadership style?
_____
_____
_____

4. You ask one of your long-time employees to take on a new task. His past performance shows that he has done well with your direction and support. The new task is important in making sure the project is completed on time. He may not have all the skills needed to do the task, but he is enthusiastic about the new challenge. You:
_____
_____
_____

What is your leadership style?
_____
_____
_____

5. Your organization has recently seen an increase in work. You have asked one of your employees to take on a new responsibility. You have worked with him for several years now, and you know that he has the knowledge and skills to be successful. However, he seems insecure about his ability to do the job. You decide to:

_____

_____

_____

What is your leadership style?

_____

_____

_____

6. You are the dean in the business department of a college that is doing well. Student success is important to you. You would like student retention to increase, and you would also like to increase graduation rates. You decide to:

_____

_____

_____

What is your leadership style?

_____

_____

_____

"It takes 20 years to build a reputation and only five minutes to ruin it. If you think about that, you will do things differently."

—Warren Buffett, billionaire investor

Warren Buffett is the business. Just as I have been a leader since I came out of the womb, so, too, has Warren Buffett. Did you know that he reads like five to six hours a day, according to some reports? Do you know what he is reading? Do you know why he reads so much? He is reading newspapers and corporate reports. His net worth is 77.7 BILLION DOLLARS. Hello, somebody. Buffett's leadership style is transformational. He has over 300,000 employees that he inspires, and whose lives are transformed by being under his leadership.

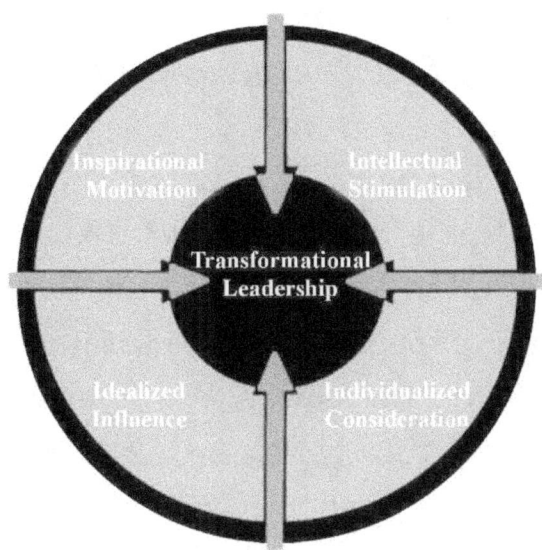

*Created by Entrepreneurship Empowered based on
Transformational Leadership Theory; Downton and Burns*

What exactly is **transformational leadership**, you ask? According to STU Online, "*Transformational leadership inspires people to achieve unexpected or remarkable results. It gives workers autonomy over specific jobs, as well as the authority to make decisions once they have been trained.*

Some of the basic characteristics of transformational leadership are inspirational, in that the leader can inspire workers to find better ways of achieving a goal; mobilization, because leadership can mobilize people into groups that can get work done, and morale, in that transformational leaders raise the well-being and motivation level of a group through excellent rapport. They are also good at conflict resolution."[32]

Just like situational leadership, transformational leadership originated in the 1970s and is still very relevant today. Buffet will quickly tell you that success doesn't have an age, which is why in almost all of his readings, you will find financial reports from 1967. Even though we are in the new millennium, we can still do and learn a lot by what has taken place in the past. The trick is to use that information wisely so that we excel and make an impact in the future. This is how you go from *startup to success*.

According to STU Online, "*transformational leaders specialize in:*

- *Working to change the system*
- *Solving challenges by finding experiences that show that old patterns do not fit or work*
- *Wanting to know what has to change*
- *Maximizing their teams' capability and capacity*"[32]

You have now come to the last activity in a very meaty chapter. I am serious about taking care of the human. Like I stated before, we are nothing without the human. We are the power. We do more together than we do alone. I believe the greatest gift I get to see is others transform right before my eyes. Others are deeply inspired by how brave I am, which, mind you, my middle name means brave, so how could I not be? Once they are inspired, they receive hope. This motivates them to get up, dust themselves off, and get to work. They find the vision and they do not let go. I am in the business of building up people. You are in the business of building up people. It is then the people who build businesses. I do not want you to ever forget how that goes. I want you to become a ridiculously amazing leader, and I want you to help others transform.

Transformational Leadership

For this activity, I want you to think about the ways you will be able to motivate staff as a leader. How are you going to motivate them? How are you going to set goals and put rewards in place? What do you believe will be important for everyone on the team to understand, and how are you going to convey that message as their leader? Just take some time to think and write what comes to you.

_____
_____
_____
_____
_____

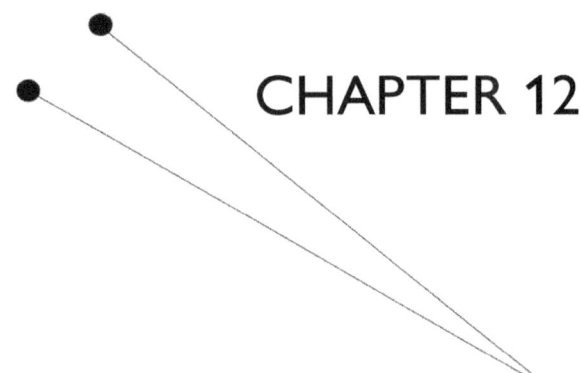

CHAPTER 12

Money Management

"If we command our wealth, we shall be rich and free. If our wealth commands us, we are poor indeed."

—Edmund Burke, philosopher

If you don't master your money, I can promise it will master you. Let me ask you a question, and I need for you to be brutally honest with yourself. How well do you handle your money? You see, the above quote is true in the sense that we will stay poor if we are commanded by our money. We have the power to command money and grow our wealth. In order to do that, we must understand how we manage our money. And, most importantly, what are limiting beliefs are about money.

I make all my students track their money. This is one of the best ways to figure out what is really going on with your finances. The longer you can track, the better. I have my students track for two weeks. However, I would say that if you can track for a month up to three months, you will have some good data. You must track it to the penny. Always keep a little book with you and don't miss one cent. Seriously, to the penny. Once you have tracked your money, you will then need to reflect and have a come-to-Jesus moment with yourself. Now, if you are already savvy and smart with your money, that's great; I would still ask you to see how you could level up and become even wiser. What little pleasures are you indulging in that could be cut so that you could further invest in yourself or your business? I am all for enjoying the simple pleasures in life, and I love luxury, but delayed gratification is a powerful tool that gives you the ability to say "no"— emotional intelligence at its finest. You should know by now that emotional intelligence is absolutely mandatory to not only go from startup to success, but to truly live the empowered life.

There are many things you need to say no to, and I need you to understand you have the right to say NO! If you wish to be matrix-free, you will need to stop feeding the matrix. Knowing how to manage your money is a must. If you don't know how to manage your money, then you surely will not know how to manage a business's money. Poor financial planning and mismanaging of funds are two of the main reasons why businesses fail. Therefore, you are going to find out right now how you manage and handle your money. Below is your first activity in this chapter—a money tracker and a space after to reflect. If you plan on going from startup to success, then you must ensure you are able to properly handle your money.

Date	Day of the week	Item(s) Purchased	Amount

Date	Day of the week	Item(s) Purchased	Amount

Now that your tracking time has come to a close, I want you to reflect and examine how you spend your money. How well do you spend money? Did you have things coming out of your account that you didn't know about? Such as a subscription that you don't use? Do you eat out every day, and is it adding up? Do you have a shopping habit? What did you discover from tracking your money? What did you learn? Reflect on everything and then create some money goals and some savings goals. Make a plan on how you will manage your money better. How are you going to be EMPOWERED with the way you handle your money?

_____
_____
_____
_____
_____
_____
_____
_____
_____
_____
_____
_____
_____
_____
_____
_____
_____
_____
_____
_____
_____
_____

"An abundance mentality springs from internal security, not from external rankings, comparisons, opinions, possessions, or associations."

—Stephen Covey, educator and author

Mindset is everything. Our minds are extremely powerful. It has taken me years upon years to rewire my mind. With regard to money, I am still learning, just like each of you. But I am certainly wiser today than I was in the past. When I first bought my business, I had a poverty mindset. I had been so poor for so long that I really didn't know how to handle the money of the business. I didn't know how to even pay myself. I just picked at the money. I bought STFF in 2002, and it wasn't until 2004 that I bought furniture for my house. I lived in a house with no living room furniture for two years, but all the while I had the money.

I can clearly remember Dan (the man I bought my business from) coming to see me for Christmas the first year I owned STFF. I had the biggest Christmas tree in the front room of my house with the most beautifully wrapped gifts underneath, and inside were some of the best gifts one could imagine. There were presents everywhere. I mean, the floor was COVERED.

Dan said, "Natasha, I love your tree, but where is your furniture?"

I kindly replied, "I'm finally able to give quality gifts to those I love."

"But what about you?" he asked.

It took me almost fifteen years from that point to finally think about me. Don't lose that much time. How old are you? Now, how long have you been subjecting yourself to the weight of others? Gifting everyone else but never gifting yourself? This was my biggest problem. I never know how to pay myself first. I had a trauma response thinking as well. I believed that if I bought people nice gifts, maybe they would love me. Maybe then I would matter. I would be worthy. Rubbish! I am worthy. I do matter. I am loved and supported, no matter what. No strings attached. A limited mindset is not what belongs to me. I have my birthright—abundance.

There is a survival mindset, and there is an abundant mindset. The survival mindset will have you forever stuck in poverty. You will steal, you will sell your body, you will do things that are unspeakable, and you will hate yourself time and time again for living in such a mindset. I lived in a survival mindset for a very long time. Then I met a wonderful woman by the name of Susan Davison. I had the honor of working side by side with her on some awesome projects, and even today, I still work with her. Susan is a financial expert. At one point in her life, she was a stockbroker. She has many stories regarding the New York Stock Exchange and what it was like to work the floor. She is also an energy worker and one of my gurus. She has given me tip after tip regarding the abundant mindset. I said to myself, *"What the hell can I lose by trying some of these tips out?"* It all starts in the mind, remember.

So, I deliberately worked on my thinking and how I spoke. I started by writing once a month about the abundance I wanted. Abundance is not just about money. I would ask for anything—from money to nail growth, to hair growth, to health, to classes, to workshops, to love, and so on. We get so hung up on money, but I demand abundance in all areas of my life. Suddenly, it was like someone poured the rain of abundance over my head, and it has yet to stop. Now I don't request the abundance; I give thanks for it. I am grateful. Gratitude is key.

My last point regarding money includes an activity which I really want you to spend some time doing. Dig deep within yourself, as that is the only way out. Limiting beliefs run and rule our world more than we acknowledge. Our thoughts become our reality, as the saying goes. No truer words for your relationship with money and the thoughts you have around it. Over the course of the year, I have spent a lot of time working with powerful female coaches. These women are making six and seven figures a month. Yes, you read that right. Six and seven figures a month. And, to top it off, they are doing this in one of the most tragic years of all—2020. A year where the world has been flipped upside down. Here are some of the top tips I have learned from these women. Money mimics. It will mimic you, your thoughts, your world. So be very careful with what you think, say, and do.

Money is really the energy of a woman. The divine feminine essence is she. Do not treat it poorly! Treat her like a lady, because she is one. She loves to feel wanted and desired. She loves to be turned into diamonds, trips, business ventures, elegant suits, dresses, and all kinds of luxury. She loves philanthropy so much! This is the energy of money when you truly tap into her. This is where she thrives, and so will you. The energy of ten million dollars has a high frequency. It feels like champagne bubbles, fireworks, and bliss. You must understand the energetics behind your work, your relationships, your life, and all you create. You must stay at a high frequency, one that is going to look very strange to those who are still sleeping. You must be okay with looking strange. You must be okay with being a rebel and breaking the rules when it comes to money. There is a pool of wealth that we all get to pull from. When we pull from that, we are not taking from anyone else. Why? Because there is plenty for all. But it is up to each person to take what they wish. This is why I teach EMPOWEREMENT. I am not the healer; I am the beacon who shines the light. I am the one who provides the tools, who leads the way, who gets in the ground with you so I can reach you. But it will be up to you to set yourself free. Freedom comes in pieces.

"When you are grateful, fear disappears and abundance appears."

—Tony Robbins, author and life coach

I knew I was in the right place by being led and taught by these women for one simple key. They are filled with gratitude, and they are truly joyful in nature and spirt. They, in essence, are me. We are coded to each other. I have awakened even more by being connected to them. As they pour into me, I turn around and pour into others. This is what it is all about. The pouring of one cup to the filling of another. This is why you must be wise in who is pouring into you. Because, truth be told, we all are being poured into and we are all pouring into others, no matter how small or how large.

I listened to what they were teaching. I took notes, I never missed a session, I showed up, I was committed, and I began working on the tasks that were given. Most importantly, I paid them. And I still do to this day. You must be willing to invest in yourself. You must also be willing to invest in others' business and not just take what's free. Free is a limited belief too. Addressing my limiting beliefs became top priority. I desired to fully walk into my abundance. I am the blue lady billionaires. My higher self. She doesn't have limited beliefs. She is the billionairess, for God's sake. She thanks me for removing the limiting beliefs. You see, it isn't until we address those beliefs and remove them once and for all that we will truly see the promise land—the land that was always ours by birthright.

Over the summer of 2019, I was able to attend a women's empowerment summit in San Diego, California. One exercise we did was a guided meditation focused on money. We were asked to allow money to show itself to us, then report on it after the meditation. When the spirit of money first appeared to me, it appeared as bare bones. It was quite odd, to say the least. Then, that body of bones quickly began to morph into the most beautiful flowing light source. Have you ever seen a butterfly costume? The ones where the sleeves are wings? When you lift your hands, the wings appear. Well, this beautiful beaming body of light had just that. As it morphed into a body of light, it lifted its hands, and wings of light appeared. It flowed with incredible energy. It told me it was bigger than bare bones and it wanted to give me more. I pondered the exercise, and I realized that due to my family history of poverty, which became my story, too, I had learned to live off bare bones. My mind was still seeing bare bones, but before me was really an ever-flowing light source of money that wanted to give me more. Abundance had appeared, and a shift took place inside my mind. Another piece of freedom had arrived.

I use this same abundance meditation in my EMPOWEREMENT workshops and many of my guest speaking appearances. Many times, what my participants see causes them to weep. It is unimaginable how amazing their personal abundance is to them. I have had them report back that large sums of money they had been waiting on for a long time finally hit their bank account right as I was closing out the meditation. I have had others report that they walked through lush landscapes and flowing rivers of abundance. I had another woman report that she saw her very own artwork lining walls and checks falling off them as she passed through. The most special of all, however, was when one of my participants saw her son who had been dead for more than seventeen years. There, at the end of the stairs, her son was waiting for her with his arms stretched and his light beaming, ready and excited to embrace her with his love. Love is the greatest of all. Love is the only thing that is real. Everything else is an illusion. Love never dies but it does transcend, as each of us will do one day. My question to you is: When are you going to truly live in your rightful birthplace? The birthplace of love and abundance? It is available to you now!

I want you to spend some time thinking about money and your relationship with it. How has your family history of money translated into your story? I encourage you to go into a meditated state to start the process and ask the spirit of money to appear to you. No pressure in how it appears, just allow what comes to come. You will find a set of questions to guide you along the way and space to write. Of all the activities, this is by far one of the most powerful ones I offer. We are rewriting your story. We are taking your power back. We are expanding your being and allowing space for the new you to arrive—the higher self. The one who is going to go from startup to success.

How did the spirit of money appear to you in your meditation, and did it have a message for you?

_____
_____
_____
_____
_____
_____
_____
_____
_____
_____
_____
_____
_____
_____
_____
_____
_____

What did you see in your family regarding money matters?

What are your current beliefs regarding money?

_____
_____
_____
_____
_____
_____
_____
_____
_____
_____
_____
_____

What would you like to see for your future regarding money?

_____
_____
_____
_____
_____
_____
_____
_____
_____
_____
_____
_____

The best way to manage your money is to come to the truth of what you do with it. Money can become a master, just like technology, so you must be careful with it and remember that you are in control. Once you take a closer look at your spending habits and become wise with your money by learning how to curb your appetite for foolish spending, you will be able to take your wisdom and place it in your business. This is how you go from startup to success—not only for your business, but for yourself!

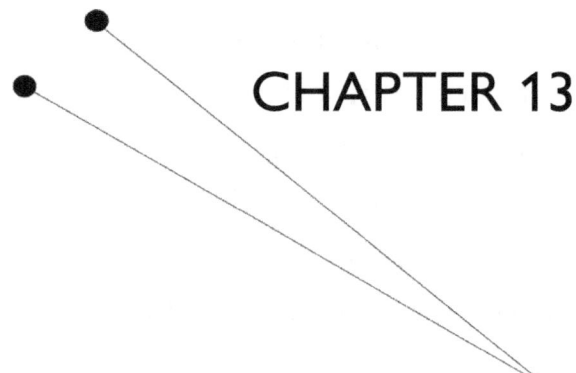

CHAPTER 13

Accounting and Taxes

"Don't ever let your business get ahead of the financial side of your business. Accounting, accounting, accounting. Know your numbers."

—Tilman J. Fertitta

Managing your money and knowing your numbers are instrumental in the control and success of your business. You will need to ensure you take great care of your financial matters. It is wise to bring in help with your financial matters. Consider hiring a certified public accountant (CPA) or bookkeeper, or use an online service. A CPA will typically cost more than online services but can normally offer more tailored services for your specific business needs. A bookkeeper can provide basic day-to-day functions at a lower cost but won't possess the formal accounting education of a CPA. Ensure that someone can manage the following:

- *Accounts receivable*
- *Accounts payable*
- *Available cash*

- *Bank reconciliation*
- *Payroll*

You will also need to manage your business credit. Establishing and managing business credit can help your company secure financing when you need it, and with better terms. Business credit can be crucial for negotiating supply agreements and protecting against business identity theft. The SBA shares five steps that can lay the groundwork to sound financial planning:

1. *"Determine whether you have business credit on file with Dun & Bradstreet*
2. *Establish a business credit history by using lines of credit associated with your business*
3. *Pay bills on time and understand other factors that influence your credit rating*
4. *Keep your credit files current and monitor for ratings changes*
5. *Know your customers' and vendors' credit standing*

Knowing your customers' credit standing gives you a window into consumer patterns, and that can affect your marketing and sales strategy. You may not need to conduct credit checks, but there are credit evaluation tools available for small business. Customer behavior also impacts your business's cash flow, which affects planning for future supplies, hiring employees, and expanding your business."[14]

A DUNS number is yet another number you will want to acquire when doing business. It is also a very simple process. DUNS stands for Data Universal Numbering System. Dun & Bradstreet are the developers and controllers of the DUNS number. It is a unique number for your business. It is used for business credit. If you plan to bid on any government proposals, you must have a DUNS number. When registering for your DUNS number, you'll need to have the following on hand:

- Legal name
- Headquarters name and address for your business

- Doing Business As (DBA) or other name by which your business is commonly recognized
- Physical address, city, state, and ZIP Code
- Mailing address (if different from headquarters and/or physical address)
- Telephone number
- Contact name and title
- Number of employees at your physical location
- Whether you're a home-based business

Now I would like for you to go to Dun & Bradstreet's website and explore. Then write down what you found in your research. Take notes. You may not wish to file for a DUNS number now, but you are collecting information to ensure you are ready when the time comes. www.dnb.com.[33]

_____
_____
_____
_____
_____
_____
_____
_____
_____
_____
_____
_____
_____
_____
_____
_____
_____
_____

Did you know the wealthy have a language all their own? Well, they do. They understand the true meaning of assets and liabilities. They speak stocks, bonds, mutual funds, and securities. They pay attention to the flow of money not only in our country, but the world. Therefore, if you are going to go from startup to success, you will need to understand the language of the wealthy. We are now going to turn our attention to some basic accounting. If you haven't taken an accounting class, I highly encourage you to do so. When I purchased STFF, Dan encouraged me to take a managerial accounting class just to give me a foundation for understanding accounting and financial planning. I now give that same recommendation to all my students and clients. I often remind my students that it is perfectly fine to hire someone smarter than you. However, don't you ever not **know your numbers**. If you don't know your accounting, someone could take advantage of you. I have seen it happen. Don't let that happen to you. Take the class, know your numbers, pay attention, and be aware of what is going on with your business numbers.

There are a few financial reports I want you to become familiar with: the *income statement*, *balance sheet*, and *cash flow*. In the back of the book, I have given charts for you to see what each one of them looks like. The **income statement** is a financial report that measures the financial performance of your business on a monthly or annual basis.

The income statement tells you just that: how much income (profit/loss) you made. As I stated in the previous paragraph, it is also called the profit and loss statement, because it will show both. I want you to always be in the black, not the red. If you haven't heard the saying *being in the black or red*, let me tell you what it means. The **black means profit**, and the **red means loss.** Some businesses do go into the red. It is common for startups to be in the red, but you don't want to stay there. You simply cannot stay there and survive in business.

The **balance sheet** is a financial report that shows what the company owes and what it owns, including shareholders' stake. The balance sheet has a particular formula which, again, must be balanced. This is the fundamental accounting equation: Assets = Liabilities + Owner's Equity. The balance sheet is going to show you the big picture, help you measure the value of your business, and can serve as an early warning sign. The balance sheet is also something that current or potential investors will want to look at and interpret. They will want to know how their investment is doing or will do.

I am sure by this point you are wondering, *What do all these different accounting terms mean?* After I introduce you to the third and final report, *cash flow*, I will be providing you with some key accounting terms. I need you to become familiar with the meanings of those terms. You can find a list of accounting terms and definitions in the back of the book for your reference, as well. The **cash flow statement** is a financial report that details the inflows and outflows of cash for a company over a set period of time. You always want to be aware of your cash flow. *Cash is king.* I know you have heard that saying before, right? If not, well, now you have. Understanding the flow of cash is critical in business. It will show you if you have enough cash on hand to pay for your current liabilities. Here is where money management really comes into play. You must know how to handle the money in the most effective and efficient way. You must be wise with your business spending habits, just as you need to be wise with your personal spending habits. The cash flow statement has three components, though not all businesses use all three:

1. *Cash from operating activities*
2. *Cash from investing activities*
3. *Cash from financing activities*

The operating activities is the most commonly used component in small business. It will consider the current expenses, as well as the current accounts receivable. The cash flow statement complements the balance sheet and income statement, and it has been a mandatory part of a company's financial reports since 1987. It's still required today in entrepreneurship.

"Nothing is certain except death and taxes."
—Benjamin Franklin

No truer statement than that from our beloved Benjamin Franklin. In order to go from startup to success, you must fully understand taxation. How you structure your business will determine what kind of taxes you will pay. The taxes will vary from business to business, but what is certain is you will pay them. And you will find them allocated in your financial reports. A word to the wise: don't fall behind on paying your taxes, and if you do, reach out to the Internal Revenue Service (IRS). They will help you. You can't get blood out of a rock, so make sure you clearly communicate with them if you are struggle financially and not able to pay. Setting aside what you owe for taxes is extremely important. Don't touch it. That is not your money! That is the government's money, and I promise Uncle Sam is coming for it.

The following information comes directly from the SBA:

"Your business is legally required to pay taxes and keep accounting records on a consistent yearly schedule called a tax year. Most businesses choose their tax year to be the same as the calendar year. You select your tax year the first time you file for taxes, but you can change it later with permission from the IRS. Calendar tax year if you don't have special accounting needs for your business. Fiscal tax year if you want your 12-month accounting cycle to end in a month that isn't December. Short tax year if your business wasn't in existence for an entire tax year, or you changed your accounting period. If your business doesn't have much reporting or bookkeeping, you might be required to use a calendar tax year. Check with the IRS for detailed rules about tax years. Your business might need to pay state and local taxes. Tax laws vary by location and business structure, so you'll need to check with state and local governments to know your business' tax obligations. The two most common types of **state and local** *tax requirements for small business are income taxes and employment taxes. Your state income tax obligations are determined by your business structure.*

For example, corporations are taxed separately from the owners, while sole proprietors report their personal and business income taxes using the same form. If your business has employees, you'll be responsible for paying state employment taxes. These vary by state but often include workers' compensation insurance, unemployment insurance taxes, and temporary disability insurance. You might also be responsible for withholding employee income tax. Check with your state tax authority to find out how much you need to withhold and when you need to send it to the state. Your business structure determines what federal taxes you must pay and how you pay them. Some of the taxes require payment throughout the year, so it's important to know your tax obligations before the end of your tax year.

There are five general types of business taxes:

1. Income tax

2. Self-employment tax

3. Estimated tax

4. Employer tax

5. Excise tax

Each category of business tax might have special rules, qualifications, or IRS forms you need to file. Check with the IRS to see which business taxes apply to you.

If your business has employees, you might be required to withhold taxes from their paychecks. Federal employment taxes include income, Social Security and Medicare, unemployment, and self-employment taxes. Check with the IRS to see which taxes you need to withhold.

Corporations have the strictest internal requirements. Corporations should hold initial and annual director and shareholder meetings, record their meeting minutes, adopt and maintain bylaws, issue stock to shareholders, and record all stock transfers.

LLCs have less strict internal requirements but are generally advised to maintain an updated operating agreement, issue membership shares, record all membership interest transfers, and hold annual meetings. Other business structures have few, if any, internal requirements. However, it's rarely a bad idea to document important decisions with your business. Your annual filing requirements will vary based on your business structure and the state. Still, there are a few common requirements to look out for.

Annual report or biennial statement. Most states require one or the other. Some states set the due date on the anniversary of the business formation date, and other states pick a specific day for all businesses. Statement filing fees. Fees normally accompany the annual report or biennial statement, which can exceed $300.00. Franchise tax. Some states charge franchise taxes for corporations or LLCs that operate within their borders. Formulas vary by state. Initial reports. Some states require initial reports and fees shortly after incorporation. Articles of Amendment. If you've made important changes to your company—like address, name, new shares, or membership—report it with articles of amendment. The documents for staying legally compliant vary based on your industry and location. Maintain any licenses, permits, or certificates your business received from your state, city, or county. Renewal requirements vary, so it's best to check with local business licensing offices."[14]

I want you now to do a little tax research. I want you to go find information on the five types of taxes: income tax, self-employment tax, estimated tax, employer tax, and excise tax. I want you to define them and then research all you can regarding them. Make notes below on all you find.

_____
_____
_____
_____
_____
_____
_____

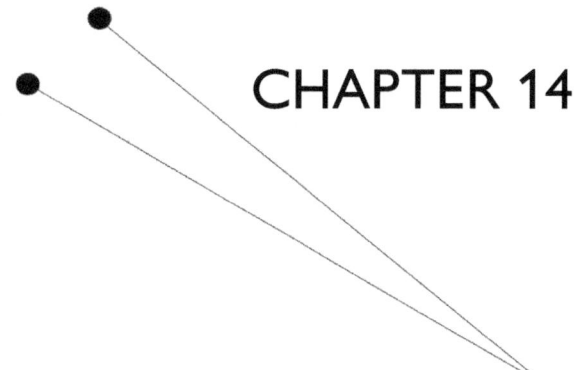

CHAPTER 14

Revenue Model and Pricing

"The revenue engine is a whole system. It encompasses a diverse set of integrated components, each doing its part to advance the system's purpose. The engine is not just comprised of marketing and sales—it includes product, accounting, and the underlying technology and data infrastructure required to keep everything flowing. It involves people, tools, workflow, and metrics. Its purpose is to optimize reach, conversion, and expansion of customer spend."

—Tom Mohr, serial entrepreneur and Fortune 500 executive

Now that you have a little more information regarding accounting, I want to dive deeper into the revenue model. A revenue model "*describes the structure of how a company generates revenue or income. Each customer segment can contain one or more revenue streams.*" As an entrepreneur, you must understand the revenue model, and you must have a revenue strategy. You are going to start by asking yourself what your revenue streams are and what your pricing is. Your streams will be the strategy, and the price will be the tactics used. Revenue streams have three questions to answer:

How much are my customers willing to pay? (This will require some research to find out what customers are willing to pay.)

How many customers do I need?
___
___
___
___
___
___
___
___
___
___
___
___

How much revenue can be generated through sales?
___
___
___
___
___
___
___
___
___
___
___

If I have more than one revenue stream, how much does each stream contribute to the total?

_____
_____
_____
_____
_____
_____
_____
_____
_____
_____
_____
_____
_____

There are many different revenue strategies. I am going to share a few with you, but I also encourage you to do additional research on this topic, as you may find a better solution for your social enterprise.

Unit sales measures the amount of revenue generated by the number of items (units) sold by a company. This is the one I used in my business. My revenue was generated by the number of files I sold. The more files I sold, the more money I made. The **subscription model** is an ever-growing strategy and, to be honest with you, it is absolutely brilliant. A subscription revenue model charges a customer for continual use of the product and or service. Do you have Netflix? Or better yet, Amazon Prime? Those are both subscription strategies. The **freemium revenue** model is one of my favorites. Who doesn't love something free? According to an article in the *Harvard Business Review* titled, "Making 'Freemium' Work," by Vineet Kumar, *"freemium'—a combination of 'free' and 'premium'—has become the dominant business model* *among internet startups and smartphone app developers. Users get basic features at no cost and can access richer functionality for a subscription fee.*"[34] The freemium model offers a product or service for free, but then you pay a premium for advanced features. Dropbox is a great example of this strategy. You get free storage up to 2GB, but then if you pay $9.99 per month for the pro plan, you can get up to 1 TB, which is significantly more space.

Fee for service model is another strategy I use. As a consultant and coach, I charge a fee for my services. I have different packages that I offer for my services, and my clients pay me by the hour. You may also want to consider using a **licensing model**. A licensing model is defined as *"a business arrangement in which one company gives another company permission to manufacture its product for a specified payment."*

As an entrepreneur, you may invent something that you will sell only the licenses to use. You will retain ownership but allow other companies the right to use your products. We have already touched on intellectual property (IP). If you are looking at the licensing model, you will want to ensure you take all the proper steps with your IP and seek legal advice.

"Price is what you pay. Value is what you get."

—Warren Buffett, CEO of Berkshire Hathaway

We just covered a few different revenue streams, and now we are going to turn our attention to pricing. This is the second part of the revenue model. Remember, people pay for value. The more you know how much people value your products or services, the better you can set your price. There are two types of pricing models: **fixed and dynamic**. Fixed is just that. It is a price that is set, and a customer will either pay the price or pass on buying. The dynamic model is not fixed, and the price is different for each customer. There are two ways to break down dynamic pricing: segmented pricing and negotiated pricing. I am sure when you read negotiated pricing, you think of car sales. That is exactly right. It is where you go back and forth until both the buyer and the seller believe they have reached a fair price. Segmented pricing, on the other hand, sells a product or service at a different price, not because of the cost to create, but rather because of the different geographical location or by the perception of the consumer.

What are some ways to set your pricing using the fixed price model? You get to decide. One of the most common ways is to do cost plus markup. You take what it costs you to make the product, and then you mark it up. For example, if it costs you $50.00 to make your product, then a general rule of thumb is to mark up 100%. You will then sell your product for $100.00. Now, if your customer holds a greater value in your product, you could set the price based on value. They may find the value in the product to be $150.00 or even $200.00, and therefore, you set your price accordingly. Another way to set your fixed price is by volume. When you set the price in volume, it is based on the number of products you buy. The more a client or customer buys, the lower the price for the product. I use this same model with my consulting and coaching. The more you buy, the lower the price for my services.

You will need to try different ways of setting your price, and you will also need to try different strategies to see which one works the best for you, your business, and even your industry. Regardless of which way you go, you will always need to ensure you are covering your cost to produce your products or service. If you are providing a service like coaching and consulting, you will need to set a price floor, meaning you cannot go any lower than a set amount or it is simply not worth your time. You need to remember to never undervalue your time and yourself. When you have a product, there will be cost in not only producing the product but running the business. You will need to understand what all your fixed costs are and what all your variable costs are. You will use those numbers to figure out your break-even point, which I will be telling you more about in just a short bit.

Below are more pricing strategies terms and definitions then some space to do some planning for your pricing.

Competition-led pricing is where prices match those of your competitors. Understand that just because you have the same price as your competitor doesn't mean a customer will buy from you. You will need to differentiate your business.

Customer-led pricing is what the customer is willing to pay. You will need to ask your target market what they think the price should be. Priceline is known for this, as they allow customers to bid on the price. They do, of course, have the power to accept or reject the price. But again, the customer is leading the price.

Loss-leader pricing sets the price below cost. This strategy is used to attract more customers. Special discounts or reducing of a price is offered in this type of strategy.

Introductory offer is a strategy where people are offered free or heavily discounted pricing to try a new product. It could be even something like the first 50 customers receive the product for 75% off.

Price skimming is when a business sets the highest initial price on a product, then lowers it over time. This is commonly used for new products or services that have very little or no competition. Bigger known innovation companies use this strategy often.

Psychological pricing is used all the time, and the consumer eats it up. To the consumer mind, anything ending in either .99 or .95 is more appealing because it gives consumers the illusion that they're saving money. Flash sales such as buy one, get one free are also ways to use the psychological pricing strategy.

Use the space provided to figure out how you are going to set your prices. Remember to reflect on your costs that are involved, both fixed and variable costs.

___
___
___
___

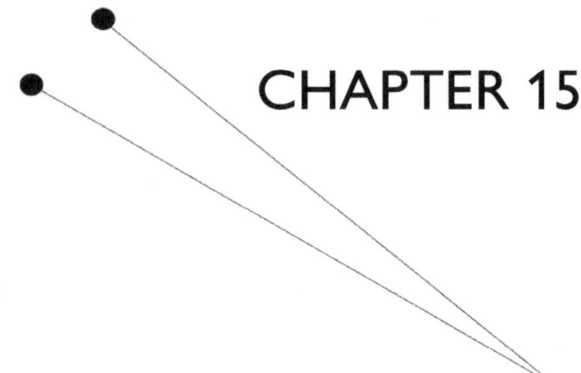

CHAPTER 15

Startup Cost, Break-Even Point, and Funding Your Business

"The startup cost of a business is paid in more than dollars and cents: It's also paid in a willingness to face fears and possibly fail and possibly soar."

—Anonymous

Another important aspect in starting a business is the cost it takes to do so. Let's break down some of the startup costs you will likely incur as a new business. Keep in mind there is no cookie-cutter recipe for businesses. Each business is going to have different needs and expenses. There is no one-size-fits-all financial solution. You are going to need to make a startup expenses worksheet. There are several different templates available that you can download and type directly into. The following are common startup costs you are likely to have, regardless of what business type:

- Office space

- Equipment and supplies
- Communications
- Utilities
- Licenses and permits
- Insurance
- Inventory
- Employee salaries
- Advertising, marketing, and market research
- Printed marketing material
- Making a website
- Lawyers and accountants

Don't underestimate your startup cost. Do your research. I would even encourage you to add 5–10% to each of your startup costs. I would rather you have excess than be short. When doing your research for startup costs, it is wise to reach out to someone who is in a similar field of business and ask them what costs they have incurred. Normally, others in business are open to speaking with aspiring entrepreneurs. If someone says no, then just keep searching until you find someone. Below is space to draft what you come up with.

_____
_____
_____
_____
_____
_____
_____
_____
_____
_____

_____
_____
_____
_____
_____
_____

We are now going to turn our attention to the break-even analysis (aka break-even point). One of the very first things Dan taught me about the business was the break-even point. Remember me stating earlier how he recommended I take a managerial class? Well, in that same conversation, he introduced me to the break-even point. He actually worked the break-even point for STFF with me in his home office in Berkeley. The business dictionary defines the break-even analysis as the "*study of the mathematical relationship between costs and sales revenue, under a given set of assumptions regarding the firm's fixed costs and variable costs. In this financial analysis, the objective is to determine (in manufacturing) the number of products that must be sold at a given price to cover the costs, or (in project financing) number of months or years required by the forecasted total net cash flow to equal estimated total project cost. An integral part of financial planning, it is performed either by using a breakeven-formula or by drawing a breakeven graph.*" It is very important that you understand what your break-even point is. You are going to need to know what all your fixed and variable costs are. Below is an example of how to figure out your break-even point. Review the example and then work on giving it a try.

Entrepreneurship Empowered has calculated that it has fixed costs that consist of its rent, depreciation of its assets, salaries, and taxes. Those fixed costs add up to $60,000. Their product is a star bookmarker. Their variable costs associated with producing the product is raw material, labor, and commissions. Variable costs have been calculated to be $0.80 per unit. The product is priced at $2.00 each. Given this information, we can calculate the break-even point for the product using the following formula: Fixed cost divided by price of product minus variable cost equals number of units needed to sell to break even.

$60,000 ÷ ($2.00 - $0.80) = 50,000 units

Using the formula for the example given, *Entrepreneurship Empowered* would need to sell $50,000 bookmarkers to break even. Now, if they raise the price of the bookmark from $2.00 to $3.95, the number of units to sell would change.

$60,000 ÷ ($3.95 - $0.80) = 19,048 units

With the price change, they don't need to sell as many. They now break even at 19,048 units sold. Let's say raising the price is not the better solution. They may then look for a way to cut costs. First, they look at their fixed cost and see right away that they can reduce their fixed cost by $10,000. Now let's see what the new break-even point would be.

$50,000 ÷ ($2.00-$0.80) = 41,666 units

See how you can play with the numbers to figure out which is the better solution? Remember to always look for efficiency in the way you spend your money. This is why you were given the task to track your money. The better you are with your personal money, the better you will be with the money of your business.

Breaking even is a good thing as long as you have included all costs in the calculations. Many times, entrepreneurs forget to pay themselves. They don't even indicate what their salary should be. They just say, "I'll pay myself later because right now, I don't have the money to pay myself." This may be true, but you still need to allocate your salary. Remember to include that in your calculation. Use the space provided to work on your break-even point.

_____
_____
_____
_____
_____
_____

"Growth is never by mere chance; it is the result of forces working together."

—James Cash Penney, JCPenney founder

If you are going to grow from startup to success, you will do so by forces of working together with others. Many times, those forces will be funding agencies. So, what are the steps to funding your business? For me, I was self-funded. I had enough money generating that I didn't need to take any loans out for STFF. I did, however, borrow money from my uncle for Italian Tans. Other than that, my businesses were completely self-funded. To self-fund your business is called *bootstrapping*, and it's one of the most common ways new businesses start and even grow their business.

What's super-hot these days is **crowdfunding**. I think many of you have already been exposed to some form of crowdfunding. Crowdfunding is used in many ways, not just business, but it seems to be most successful in business. The word tells you about its meaning: a crowd of people come together to fund your business. Crowdfunding is not a loan. The money you receive doesn't need to be paid back. In some cases, it is like a prepayment for your product or service. In others, it is more an offering of support in exchange for some swag, which could be a T-shirt, a coffee cup, or the like. The Crowdfunding Centre's May 2014 report identified two primary types of crowdfunding:

1. *Rewards crowdfunding: entrepreneurs pre-sell a product or service to launch a business concept without incurring debt or sacrificing equity/shares.*
2. *Equity crowdfunding: the backer receives shares of a company, usually in its early stages, in exchange for the money pledged.*

The SBA has some really awesome tutorials regarding crowdfunding. I highly recommend you take a look at them. One of the colleges I teach at is in Grass Valley, California—a very small town with a lot of charm and character. I bring in one of the local business owners to speak to my students about crowdfunding. She owns a restaurant called Three Forks Bakery & Brewing Co. She was able to raise $45,000 through crowdfunding. Her success with crowdfunding is incredible. She shares her story not only with my students, but with other business professionals in the town, and she has been instrumental in helping and starting crowdfunding campaigns. All of that results in receiving large sums of money.

She will tell you, and so will I, that you must have a really good story. People want to hear your story. They also want to see that you are invested. If you are not invested in your own business, how do you expect someone else to be invested? That sounds silly, but you would be surprised how many people are not invested. They, however, are not empowered entrepreneurs. So, tell your story. What's your background? What are your dreams for your business? This will help humanize and frame your case. Share your achievements and progress. What have you invested in your business already?

There are other ways to fund your business. I have now given you information on two of four ways: number one, self-funding; number two, crowdfunding. The third and fourth ways are through loans and investors. **Loans** are a lump sum of money you receive, commonly from a bank or other financial institution. You pay back loans with interest. The SBA backs 80% of the small business loans in the United States. They don't lend you the money; remember, they only back you. You must be credit-worthy for any loan. Your business must be in good financial standing and have a solid foundation. Typically for a business loan, you need a traditional business plan, which must include an expense sheet and financial projections for up to five years. Now, if your credit is not right and your business is not in good financial standing, then please don't waste your time. You will not get a loan. It is as simple as that.

There are two types of **investors**: angel investors and venture capitalists. An angel investor is normally a wealthy person who provides funding to a business startup in exchange for convertible debt or ownership equity. Angel investors are often retired entrepreneurs or executives who may be interested in angel investing for reasons that go beyond pure monetary return. These include wanting to keep abreast of current developments in a particular business arena, mentoring another generation of entrepreneurs, and making use of their experience and networks on a less-than-full-time basis. Thus, in addition to funds, angel investors can often provide valuable management advice and important contacts.

Venture capitalists, on the other hand, provide funding after an initial seed funding has already been given. Seed funding could come from crowdfunding or an angel investor. Venture capitalists commonly take on high-risk companies for a high return. A venture capitalist is a person who makes venture investments, and these venture capitalists are expected to bring managerial and technical expertise, as well as capital, to their investments. A venture capital fund refers to a pooled investment vehicle (in the United States, often an LP or LLC) that primarily invests the financial capital of third-party investors in enterprises that are too risky for the standard capital markets or bank loans. These funds are typically managed by a venture capital firm, which often employs individuals with technology backgrounds (scientists, researchers), business training, and/or deep industry experience.

I am now going to close this chapter out on startup seed funding. There are three different types of seed funding in the startup world: Series A, B, and C. According to Investopedia, "*Series A financing refers to an investment in a privately-held, startup company after it has shown progress in building its business model and demonstrates the potential to grow and generate revenue. Initially, startup companies rely on small investors for seed capital to begin operations. Seed capital can come from the entrepreneurs and founders of the company (a.k.a., friends and family), angel investors, and other small investors seeking to get in on the ground floor of a potentially exciting new opportunity. Crowdsourcing is another way for angel investors to access investment opportunities in startups. The main difference between seed capital and Series A funding is the amount of money involved and what form of ownership or participation the investor receives. Seed capital will usually be in smaller amounts (e.g., tens or hundreds of thousands of dollars), while Series A financing is typically in the millions of dollars. Series A financing comes from well-established venture capital (VC) and private equity (PE) firms, such as D.E. Shaw and Kleiner Perkins, which manage multi-billion-dollar portfolios of multiple investments in startup and early development companies.*

Series B financing is the second round of funding for a business through investment, including private equity investors and venture capitalists. Successive rounds of financing a business are consecutively termed Series A, Series B, and Series C financing. The Series B round generally takes place when the company has accomplished certain milestones in developing its business and is past the initial startup stage. In a Series B financing round, companies have advanced their business, resulting in a higher valuation by this time. Companies can seek various ways to raise funds in a Series B financing round. Series B investors usually pay a higher share price for investing in the company than the earlier investors through the Series A financing round. Series A financing involves capital raising for startups with a solid business model. Series A funds are usually from private equity firms and are used to expand operations by buying equipment and inventory as well as hiring staff. Series A funding is considered seed capital since it's designed to help new companies grow. Series B financing is the next stage of funding after the company has had time to generate revenue from sales. Investors have a chance to see how the management team has performed and whether the investment is worth it or not. As a result, Series B financing tends to have less risk associated with it versus Series A financing. However, Series A financiers get in at a lower share price to help compensate for that risk.

Businesses that make it to Series C funding sessions are already quite successful. These companies look for additional funding in order to help them develop new products, expand into new markets, or even to acquire other companies. In Series C rounds, investors inject capital into the meat of successful businesses, in an effort to receive more than double that amount back. Series C funding is focused on scaling the company, growing as quickly and as successfully as possible. One possible way to scale a company could be to acquire another company. Imagine a hypothetical startup focused on creating vegetarian alternatives to meat products. If this company reaches a Series C funding round, it has likely already shown unprecedented success when it comes to selling its products in the United States. The business has probably already reached targets coast to coast. Through confidence in market research and business planning, investors reasonably believe that the business would do well in Europe. Perhaps this vegetarian startup has a competitor who currently possesses a large share of the market. The competitor also has a competitive advantage from which the startup could benefit. The culture appears to fit well as investors and founders both believe the merger would be a synergistic partnership. In this case, Series C funding could be used to buy another company. As the operation gets less risky, more investors come to play. In Series C, groups such as hedge funds, investment banks, private equity firms, and large secondary market groups accompany the type of investors mentioned above. The reason for this is that the company has already proven itself to have a successful business model; these new investors come to the table expecting to invest significant sums of money into companies that are already thriving as a means of helping to secure their own position as business leaders. Most commonly, a company will end its external equity funding with Series C."[35]

The more you can learn about the ecosystem of the startup world, specifically regarding how they are funded, the stronger you will become and the better you will be able to navigate the startup world. I highly suggest doing your research to gain all the knowledge you can. The best knowledge is experience, and I encourage you to take the leap and go from startup to success.

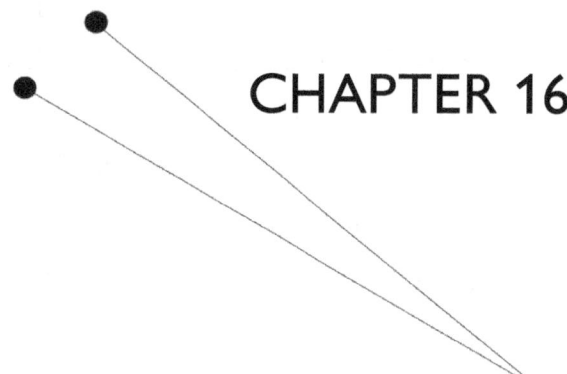

CHAPTER 16

The Secret to Success

"Success is not a secret, it is a system."

—Florence Shinn, American artist

You see, my dear ones, there is no secret to success. But there is a system, and each person has their own system that is coded to them, for them. Take a big deep breath with me now. Come on.... BIG DEEP BREATH. Release and sit in this truth: You were born into this lifetime for a purpose. You have a calling on your life and you will fulfill it if you faint not. It is not going to be easy. And as the saying goes, nothing worth having is easy. It will take work and hard work at that. But then there will come a time when you will have a season of ease. And from this place you will awaken even more to the truth that all things work to the good. That indeed you have been chosen. That your harvest has at last come in. We climb to the mountaintop not because that is where we are going. Oh no! We climb so we can see the promised land. Then we go take possession of it. This is the journey you are on.

I have been very excited to write this chapter because I am leaving you with the best advice I can offer. I am going to share what I use in my system, and perhaps some of what I use will work for you. But remember, some of it may not. You will have your own system to create. What I want most is for you to know that you are now EMPOWERED to create that system. Because the greatest gift I give to others is the gift of self. Once you have *you* back, everything else falls into place. Everything you need you will find within. The deeper we crawl within, the freer we become. The freer we are, the more powerful we become. Freedom, just like healing, comes in pieces. And before you know it, the puzzle of your life comes together to make the most beautiful picture of all.

Let us start by defining the word "***system***." The dictionary has two definitions for system:

1. "*a set of things working together as parts of a mechanism or interconnecting network.*"
2. "*a set of principles or procedures according to which something is done; an organized framework or method.*"

You are going to be creating your structure, your method of how you do things. You are going to do this by trial and error. Betta to be better is what I say. You are also going to do this by learning all you can. Knowledge is power. You are to be a researcher and always be thinking critically. Open your mind, then open it some more. Remember, the ultra-limits of your life is where you find the truest you yet. Go there and go there often. You will need to be anchored to yourself and know what works for you and what doesn't. You may not be a morning person. If that's the case, don't buy into this notion that "successful people are early birds." This is not true. The early bird doesn't always get the worm. I am a night owl, and I can promise you this much: I caught my worm. I might have even caught two or three of them. Then I went to bed. And if I greet the rising sun, dancing in its golden rays of yellow and orange, it's normally while I'm sitting on the beach. Or in the middle of a Sedona vortex. Or somewhere at the edge of the ultra-limits. It's an experience that turns into a memory. And it's a place of rest—or better yet, awakening. Not a place of work. This is indeed part of my system. Rest and awakening are instrumental in the journey of success. So, understand your energy and mange it well. Discovery of self is the key. I understand my energy level and how I work best. I respect myself enough to stop trying to fit into a mold that doesn't fit me. I am one of a kind, and so are you! This is what is so beautiful about being human. No two of us are the same, not even identical twins.

"I love those who can smile in trouble, who can gather strength from distress, and grow brave by reflection. 'Tis the business of little minds to shrink, but they whose heart is firm, and whose conscience approves their conduct, will pursue their principles unto death."

—Leonardo da Vinci, Renaissance genius

The quote above is right on the money. I want you to smile in the face of trouble. The distress will only make you stronger. Your bravery will be rewarded. And I want you to build a set of principles to live by. To build from. They are a part of your system. They will be the reason for your success.

I am now going to share with you my 10 Core Palumbo Principles, which I personally pursue unto death. And I'm a radical believer, so not only do I believe these principles will live with me throughout my lifetime, but in building my final empire, which is the Eternal Enterprise, I believe I will capture eternal life, and no longer will these principles be pursued only unto death. I am confident they will be shared with the world and, more importantly, they will guide my seeds into seeds forevermore. This, my friends, is how you not only break generational curses, this is also how you plant generational blessings. Below are the 10 Core Palumbo Principles, and I am going to dive deeper into four of them. I believe the four you see bolded are the most relevant for going from startup to success.

- Palumbo Principle 10: Pay Yourself First
- Palumbo Principle 9: Emotional Intelligence Is Key
- Palumbo Principle 8: Stay Gritty
- Palumbo Principle 7: Execution Is Required at All Times
- Palumbo Principle 6: **We Don't Predict Our Future; We Create It**
- Palumbo Principle 5: **Sacrifice to Succeed**
- Palumbo Principle 4: The Four Agreements
- Palumbo Principle 3: The Story of the Star
- Palumbo Principle 2: **You Have Rights to Your NO, and Your YES Is Undeniable**
- Palumbo Principle 1: **The Way Out Is Within**

"Infuse your life with action. Don't wait for it to happen. Make it happen. Make your own future. Make your own hope. Make your own love."

—Bradley Whitford, actor

Palumbo Principle 6: We Don't Predict Our Future; We Create It

The sixth principle is one of my favorites because not only do I have the ability to be creative, I also have a vast imagination. I have vision for lifetimes. I love the fact that, as an empowered entrepreneur, I will not predict my future, but rather I will create it, and that is indeed what I have been doing.

Prediction is unsure, but creation is a matter of fact. When you are creating, I want you to do more than just visualize. I want you to engage your senses. You see, when we bring the heart and the head together, there is nothing we cannot have or do. If you desire rain, don't just think about it and see it…. I need you to feel the rain on your face. I need you to smell the rain. I need you to walk around in your rain gear. This is how you activate a higher vibrational pull, and what you desire will come chasing after you. I have all kinds of vision boards—from poster boards to virtual ones that I keep on my phone. I am constantly making them. I put no time limit on the vision because, remember, though it may tarry, it is never late. It will be right on time. The vision is already ready. But it waits on you to be ready. It waits on divine alignment, which is exactly what you want it to do.

This book and all the other books that I will write are displayed on vision boards. The car I am currently driving was on a vision board. The money I am receiving from being a paid teacher is on a vision board. My wedding and marriage are on a vision board. And I promise you, the list goes on and on. I have one vision board right now manifesting at what seems to be the speed of light. So many things have all come to pass from this one vision board. What I can tell you is, I have become more aware of using my senses to feel my vision, as well as see it. This could well be the reason this one board is appearing ever so quickly. That and, well, I am ready. I am ready to truly receive what I desire.

Creating your future is true not only for personal life, but for business life as well. I was going to take over the U.S. with STFF, my core business. I stated before how I had marketing materials that were magnets the shape of the U.S., with my logo and my name and contact information on them. I also had other fact sheets that I would send out to my clients and to potential clients, which also had the U.S. on them. I was serious. I was coming for it. I didn't do too badly, truth be told. I captured 10% of the U.S. Imagine that. A welfare mom who became the CEO of her own company and went on to capture 10% of the U.S. I promise you, I did not predict that, nor could I have. But I sure had the vision to create it.

I will still take the other 90% of the U.S., and I plan to capture the globe as well. Both the U.S. and the globe are on several of my vision boards. I have seen myself traveling the world, speaking to seas upon seas of people, being the healer that I am. I know without a shadow of a doubt that I am the next top female speaker in the world and an award-winning author. This, too, is on a vision board. It is not only on a vision board, but I see it and feel it with my senses. My heart and my mind are in one accord. My vibrational level is elevated. I radiate at a very high frequency, which draws to me what I desire.

You can do the same. You must simply believe. You must remove the self-censor, which is in the center of your forehead. Do it now. Take your hand and place it on your forehead and grab it like you are going to pull your forehead off…but please don't do that, just play along. Grab your forehead and remove the self-censor. Just pull it off and throw that sucker away. Allow your creativity to take over. Believe in yourself and your vision. You don't need anyone else's approval to believe in yourself. And if you feel like you do need approval, you have just now been Professor Palumbo Approved! Boom! I want you to never stop building your vision boards, however you see fit to create them. I want you to always keep your head and heart in one accord when creating your future. It is the new millennium now. You are actually in the future because it is now.

Palumbo Principle 5: Sacrifice to Succeed

To be the crème de la crème of empowered entrepreneurs, you must understand that you will have to sacrifice in order to succeed. You will have to sacrifice sleep, food, relationships, parties, events, movies, news events, family time, and the like. This is what it will take for you to rise to the top. You will make the sacrifice, and if you have a family, they will need to be aware that not only are you going to make sacrifices, but they will, too. This can be the tricky part, especially for those of you who are married or have a significant other. If your spouse or partner is not on board with your vision and the direction you are going, you will need to figure out a way to get them on board. For your children, you will need to help them understand that the sacrifice will be well worth it in the end. That what you are doing is going to benefit them as well.

I am a firm believer in balance, so even though I have made many sacrifices, I have also made sure not to lose too much of myself and my time with my children. Everything else, however, I gave up. I don't watch TV. I don't even watch the news. (I do read—a lot.) I don't go out to parties. When others are partying it up on Friday or Saturday nights, I am grinding, or I am working out. I don't socialize, other than networking events to build my brand and business. I don't get caught up in family drama, and I have let go of several members of my family. I am a firm believer that *"family, friend, or foe—if they are toxic, you must let them go."* Unfortunately, too many of my family members are toxic, so I gave myself the gift of goodbye. I did this with friendships and with my foes. So many people are afraid to be alone, but being with abusive people is much worse than being alone. You are going to have to make the sacrifice to let them go and trust your vision. Trust where you are going and the purpose of your life.

There are many sayings out there along the lines of, "*You need to sacrifice like others will not in order to live like most never will.*" This is so true. So many people will never even leave their backyard. Now, this isn't a bad thing if they are free and can take themselves to the ultra-limits while sitting in their backyard; for me, however, I could never just sit in my backyard. Nor would I. I can't sit still as it is, let alone in a yard. I need to be exposed to everything I possibly can. I desire to grow in culture and in character. I am planning for a hundred generations, if not more. In order to plan for that many generations, I must make the sacrifices. I cannot play around like others do; I must be working. The grind never stops.

I love holidays—not so much for the holiday itself, but for the fact that I get to grind. So, when I do desire to take a trip, I can do so without even blinking an eye. Which is exactly what I am about to do—my daughter and I are heading to Rome! I cannot tell you how many holidays I have worked and how many sleepless nights I have had, grinding and building. But today I am reaping the fruit, and it only makes me hungrier. I am able to live now and still grind at the same time.

Emotional intelligence. Delayed gratification in action. I want you to think for a moment or two on what you know you need to sacrifice right now in order to succeed. Some of you need to really let go of some people and things in your life. It is not a sacrifice so much as a way to set yourself up, so you can level up. In the space provided, I want you to list all that comes to mind regarding letting go and sacrificing. I want you to start by asking yourself: *What do I really want from life? What am I willing to stop and start to get what I want for my life? Who's counting on me?* Answer those questions and write what comes to mind for sacrifice and letting go.

_____
_____
_____
_____
_____
_____
_____
_____
_____
_____
_____
_____
_____
_____
_____
_____
_____
_____
_____
_____
_____
_____
_____
_____

Palumbo Principle 2: You Have Rights to Your NO, and Your YES Is Undeniable

Did you know that you have rights to your "no"? Many people don't know this simple truth. For me, my "no" was taken at the age of three. My "no" was stolen. I didn't know how to say, *"No, don't touch me." "No, don't beat me." "No, don't treat me like that." "No, you can't have my money." "No, I can't take you there or here or everywhere."* And if you told me no, I would be absolutely crushed. *"No, I don't love you." "No, I can't help you." "No, you didn't get that job."* And so on.

But then I became *EMPOWERED* and took the rights to my life back, which included taking rights to my "no" back! I realized I let people walk all over me because I needed to feel like I belonged; that I was loved. But that was not love at all, and it only made me sicker. The side effects of abuse are nothing nice. My trauma side effects almost killed me. But God saw me through, and He will see you through. I stopped being a people pleaser. I started saying "no" to others and "yes" to me. I became *EMPOWERED* and took my rights back. Being told "no" means nothing to me anymore because my YES is undeniable.

My ability to say "no" now has made me grow so much. I am much more balanced and healthier. Here's what is interesting: because I have started saying "no," I am able to serve at a much higher level than before. I have much more to offer in the right way, in a healthy way, and with complete purity of heart. I encourage you all to remember that you have rights to your "no," and your "yes" is undeniable. There is a time and a season for everything under the sun and in heaven. Your undeniable "yes" is found many times throughout your life and will certainly be found in heaven. You just need to allow that to remain at the forefront of your mind at all times. Your "yes" is far more powerful and purposeful than any "no" you will ever receive. As I stated before, I would be crushed to receive a "no," but my journey to becoming a professor is where I realized that my "yes" is undeniable. This powerful principle changed my life. I use this principle when I am creating my vision. I bring my senses in along with it and feel my undeniable "yes." I feel its power and purpose. I can see the "yes" appearing here and there. I know nothing is going to stop my "yes." Only I can stop it, and far too often, people do, because they don't know how to move past the "no" they just received.

As an empowered entrepreneur, you will be told "no" time and time again. These are the dice of life. But you are going to pick up those dice in your hands, shake them up, spit on them if you must, then throw them back to this world with all you have in you and say, "MY YES IS UNDENIABLE!" The power belongs to you.

Palumbo Principle 1: The Way Out Is Within

You are more powerful than you could even possibly imagine. *The way out is within.* No one is coming to save you. It is just that real. You can, however, save yourself. You were created in the image of the Most High God. Then He so graciously placed His lips on yours and blew breath into you. You are the image of God, and you have His breath in your lungs. What more do you really need?

For so many years, I wandered in the wilderness, searching and searching. One day, I came upon a large wooden door, and carved in the door in gigantic lettering was the word *VALIDATION. Oh boy,* I thought, *that is exactly what I need.* So, I knocked on the door, and all of a sudden, a guard appeared.

"What do you want?" the guard asked.

"Oh, I just want to come through this door."

"NO," the guard yelled back. "Go away."

I hung my head and away I walked. But I was determined to go through that door, so I thought to myself, *The guard will take an offering, I am sure. I will go get everything I can find. I will go dig up gold with my bare hands. I will search and collect, and I will search and collect some more, then I will take all that I have, all that I am, and give them to the guard.* I returned to the door and knocked. The guard appeared.

"What do you want?"

"I have everything I could gather. I have all the gold I could dig up, I have everything I possess, and I will give it all to you if you just let me through the door."

The guard took everything I had, then said, "NO, now go away. You cannot come through the door."

I then began to reflect: *Why am I the only one at the damn door? Where is everyone else?* The moment I had that epiphany, the guard stood up and pulled off a mask it was wearing to reveal to me who it really was. The damn guard was me.

We walk in the valley of validation and travel in the forest of falsehood, only to finally realize that the door we so desperately want to walk through, we are guarding ourselves. *The way out is within.* You must pull the mask off, take a cold, hard look at yourself, and decide that you will no longer seek approval from those who will turn to dust just like you. We all die, my friends. Not one of us gets to stay, nor do I believe we would really want to, truth be told. But I am a firm believer we can build something that will outlast time. This is why I work so hard. This is why I am determined to share with the world what I know and the keys I have used to be free.

I need you to no longer underestimate your willpower. I need you to turn your "I wish" into "I will." Stop making wishes and blowing hot air everywhere. Change your wish to "I will" and then execute. Many of you are still waiting for a wish to come true when all you have to do is go make it happen. I am a firm believer that anything is possible, and wishes do come true. But you must be action-oriented. The power of will is extremely important to understand and activate at the highest vibrational frequency. How did God create the world? His WILL. Will is all the power that exists. We don't use enough of it. We become lazy and say a wish or two instead of working our God-given power to manifest the miracles in our life. Once you recognize that your willpower is your God-given power, it will increase and show you more than you could ever begin to wish for.

"The way out is within."

—Natasha M Palumbo, author and speaker

The final activities you will do are the most powerful ones of all my activities. You are coming up to one of two of them. I am preparing you to leave me, and my confidence is that you leave much differently than when you came. I am sending you out the door EMPOWERED! The dictionary defines empowered as "*made (someone) stronger and more confident, **especially in controlling their life and claiming their rights.***" In the space provided, you are going to write your personal empowerment statement. You will also set three goals: a three-month goal, six-month goal, and one-year goal. I have provided my empowerment statement and goals as examples.

For your empowerment statement, I want you to tell me what area in your life you would like to be more *EMPOWERED*. What steps will you take to become more *EMPOWERED*? Then move into goal setting. Be realistic, but let it be a bit of a challenge. Remember, *the way out is within*, and freedom comes in pieces.

Empowered Statement—My Example:

I am a people-pleaser, and many times have become so hurt by family, friends, and people in general. What I am learning is that it is very unhealthy to be a people-pleaser. It can actually make you sick and has many times made me sick. The side effects of abuse are nothing nice. Being a people-pleaser is one of my side effects. But I am healing and will continue to heal and be free. I have decided to be *EMPOWERED* and no longer subject myself to people-pleasing. I will choose to say "no" and have no remorse. I will say "YES" to me. I am confident in myself and the purpose of my life. I know that I am not able to please everyone, nor will I inspire everyone, but I have had visions where I have seen seas upon seas of people who will be inspired by my life story. I will be used to give hope to so many that feel hopeless. I will be used to help heal and set others free. This pleases me.

Goals:
    3-month: Run a 10K
    6-month: Take a vacation
    1-year: Lose 25 pounds

Now, it is your turn....

_____

_____

_____

_____

_____

_____

_____

_____

_____

_____

_____

_____

_____

_____

_____

_____

_____

_____

_____

"Step out of the history that is holding you back. Step into the new story you are willing to create."

—Oprah Winfrey, business tycoon

In entrepreneurship, we don't predict our future using history; we create it by going to the ultra-limits of our lives by believing in our natural talents and abilities, which have been bestowed upon us by God. By now, I am hoping you have been able to discover more of who you are. I am sure by now you can see the chapters of this book have weaved in and out of self-awareness. Because it all boils down to "self." No matter which way you look or go, at the core is "self." Many times, you need to get out of your own way. I want you to imagine, if you will, a bird perched on a pier railing resting upon the seashore. The most beautifully colored blue and gray wings raised, ready for flight, but little yellow feet still stuck to the railing. The bird is ready for flight, but if it doesn't release its grip from the railing and activate its wings, it will only stand there looking silly with its wings up. My questions to you are: Are you ready to take flight? Do you know where you are going? Are you prepared? If your answers are "no," then you need to get to work. But if your answers are "yes," then what are you waiting for? Why are your wings up but feet stuck to the ground? Is it fear of failure? Which, mind you, we make up. There really is no failure. Falling on your face is fantastic; I encourage it. Faith is dead without works, but if you do the work, don't let your faith die because of fear. Many people do the work and work hard, but then never activate their wings and launch because they fear falling on their face.

I have a friend who is part of a wonderful community I am in. He lost his legs in the military. Today he is a speaker and a phenomenal one at that. He tells the story of when he got his new legs, how the doctor began working with him. His very first therapy session with his new legs was not what he was expecting, to say the least. The rails he held onto as he moved forward, step by step, disappeared into the ground. The minute they disappeared into the ground and he had nothing to hold on to, he fell forward and landed on his face. He was so angry with the doctor. He said to the doctor, "See, I told you this wasn't going to work, I just fell on my face. You don't know what you're doing." The doctor said, "I am teaching you how to walk, now get up and let's try this again." Today, this same man doesn't just walk, but he runs marathons, triathlons, and a host of other very challenging sporting events. But first, he had to fall flat on his face.

Many of you desire to be an empowered entrepreneur, you desire to go from startup to success, but you fear falling on your face. Don't do yourself an injustice. Don't throw away all the time you spent working on a business model or plan and put your wings up only to stay stuck to the ground because you fear falling. Falling is a part of the process. You need to fall. You don't learn by hitting the bullseye; you learn by missing the mark. And you will never learn if you don't release your grip and activate your wings.

"I love the recklessness of faith. First you leap, and then you grow wings."

—William Sloane Coffin, American chaplain and peace activist

Before I close out this chapter, I would like to take the time to express my gratitude to you. I am extremely grateful to you for being with me on this journey. I am confident that no matter what direction you decide to take in life, you will make an IMPACT. I am honored that you would read my writing, and if you are one of my students, I want you to know how incredibly honored I am to be your professor. To walk with you and support you on your educational journey. I believe I have given you all a wealth of information in this book. I hope you will come back time and time again to use what has now been revealed to you. What I love about being an author is, in my writings, I have found eternal life. I am confident my work will be shared with the world and, more importantly, it will guide my seeds into seeds forevermore. As I wrote earlier, this, my friends, is how you not only break generational curses, but this is how you plant generational blessings.

It took me many years to finally pull the muzzle off my mouth and live out loud. I have extraordinary God-given talents, and though I may look insane on all levels on my mansion, I have the Willy Wonka of all elevators. I promise you want to get in. Because this elevator of mine not only can go in any direction, it breaks through glass ceilings. Let that breathe for just a minute. I am a disruptor. I am proud to be that. I disturb demons. Listen, I have disturbed my own so much that they had to flee. I know that not all will like me or love me. But I am confident in myself and the purpose of my life. I am a truth speaker, a catalyst for change, and activator, and an inspiration to many. Not all will love me, true enough, but as I have written prior, I have seen seas upon seas of people coming for me to speak over and to stop the bleeding. I am going to look different—that is the whole point. Be confident in being the disruptor. I want you to get comfortable looking strange to a sleeping world. If you truly awaken, you will be very strange. But remember, they are asleep, and you have touched the hand of God. You have tapped into the source of all sources. You tap into the power of the now.

We are always in the now. That is the only door open. The past door is locked. The future door is locked. I need you to stop wasting your only open door by beating on doors that are closed. I need you to learn how to heal from the door of the past and be free from it. The future is also locked, but in moments of stillness, in moments of elevation, you lift from the now and enter a different realm. It takes time to master this. The more you practice it, the stronger you will become. Eventually, you will transcend to teacher. And teach, you must!

Let's dive deeper into the now. You catch a plane in San Francisco that takes you to Chicago, then on to London, finally landing in Africa. You never leave the plane. You start in one place but end up in another place. This, my dear one, is life. The entire plane ride, you are in the now. There really is no yesterday, nor is there a tomorrow. The now is the plane. You cannot leave the plane until you arrive at your destination. Along the plane ride, turbulence takes place. This turbulence scares you because it is lasting too long.

This doesn't seem normal. You call the flight attendant over. You express your concern. He or she tells you that there is an empty seat under the wing. Turbulence is usually not as bad under the wing. But you cannot get off the plane. You move and sit under the wing. And, indeed, the turbulence settles a bit. But you can still feel it.

"He shall cover you with His feathers, and under His wings shall you trust; His truth shall be your shield and buckler."

—Psalms 91:4

The turbulence of life comes, and we cannot get off the plane. We don't leave the now—not in physical form, at least. But we can sit under the wing. Even then, we must trust. We must hold faith that the turbulence will subside. As you call the flight attendant over another time to address the concern of the turbulence, he or she tells you not to worry, the pilot is going to take us to a higher elevation, and the turbulence will fade. Your response needs to be THANK YOU because gratitude opens the door to the now that already exists. This has been key for me in activating my abundance. I no longer ask for abundance; I give thanks for it. I give thanks for not only my abundance, but my vision. I give thanks for the turbulence and all the suffering I have endured. It has given me a story to share. It has given me the power to inspire others and help them break free. I know that I have been called to turn tragedy and trauma into TRIUMPH.

Right now, I want you to say THANK YOU. Thank you first to yourself for all you have endured in this life to date. I want you to say thank you for all you desire to have. Give thanks for your life right now. Rejoice. You have been chosen to be here in the NOW.

Let us turn our attention to the final activity. The most powerful of all, the writing of a legacy letter. Writing a legacy letter is one of the hardest things I have ever done. While earning my master's degree, a professor gave us the assignment to write a legacy letter. I had never heard of such a thing. I can clearly see myself weeping like a baby at my desk as I wrote my son a final goodbye. You see, that is what a legacy letter is. It is a letter from you to your legacy—to your family and friends. You project yourself to your deathbed and you write. It can be very hard, emotionally, because no matter how strong your faith is, the sting of death is very real. We all will cross it one day. I am a true believer that love is the only thing that is real; everything else is an illusion. Love never dies, but it does transcend, as each of us will do one day. I believe we have been given one commission here on earth, and that is to love, and we screw it up every day and three times on Sunday. This is why I share my message. This is why I live out loud. This is why the EMPOWERED series is within me. It is in my writings that I get to live—and the same is true for you. So, I encourage you to write. I desire to see you live the EMPOWERED LIFE. This is why I give you key after key to help set you free. Though this call-to-action activity is hard and may be difficult to do, I encourage you to write the letter. Go to your deathbed, what type of life did you live? What do you want to say to your children and loved ones? What do you wish to say to the future generations still yet to come? What stories, values, wisdom, and blessings do you wish to share? Just write what comes to you. Again, I thank you for being on this journey with me. I pray that you write the letter and receive yet another key. Remember, the way out is within. Go within and write the letter, then go and live the EMPOWERED LIFE.

Personal Empowered Life Legacy Letter:

_____
_____
_____
_____
_____
_____
_____
_____

Welfare to Wealth Story

"The man who understands how something is done will always be employed. The man who understands why something is done, will always be the boss of the man who only knows how. But the woman who owns the company and bends the arch of sexism understands the true and ultimate power of ambition."

—Ronald T. Hickey, author

I come from a deep history of poverty, abuse, and neglect. I have faced more in the first two decades of my life than most humans ever will. But I am a LION. Did you know that the world we live in is a jungle? There are all kinds of animals in this jungle, and you will need to familiarize yourself with all of them—especially if you desire to be successful in business. You will either eat or be eaten. It is up to you to decide which one you are going to do or be.

I am the first in my family to hold a master's degree, let alone be a woman in that category. I have been chosen in this life to be a generational curse breaker and a generational blessing maker. I have worked extremely hard and will always work hard for all that I desire. That is the key to business. Hard work pays off. Doing what you love is possible. Dreams can become a reality. Nothing is impossible.

In 1999, I began working for Start To Finish Files, a California-based legal and medical copy service that specializes in Social Security disability law. I was hired by Dan Acland, who founded the business in 1994. This man changed the entire direction of my life. Little did I know at that time that I would become the owner of Start To Finish Files. At that time, I was going to school to be a high school photography teacher. I have a K-12 education background, which serves me well today. Dan hired me on the spot. When I started at his company, I used to push around a gurney with a small copy machine on it. You should have seen me trying to get this big gurney around places. It was hilarious! And you can only imagine the looks I got. But it was a job, and it had a lot of flexibility, which worked perfectly for me while I attended school.

Dan hired me to work at the Sacramento and Stockton locations. He had four other locations in the Bay Area that he handled with another employee. In 2002, Dan came to me and told me he was going to sell the business. He was planning on returning to school to work on his PhD in economics. I, at the time, was a welfare mom. I didn't make much money working because it was only a part-time gig and I was going to school. I had no money to buy the business. I tried to look for resources to help me purchase it but to no avail.

But did you know that one moment can change a thousand after it? Well, here was that one moment for me. One Sunday morning, Dan called. I answered the phone, and I will never forget what he said: "*Natasha, I am going to sell you the business. I am selling it to you for $20,000, and I will give you $4,000 start-up cash—$2,000 one month, and $2,000 the next month. I have you set up for a two-year payment plan. I have a small interest that will be included, and I have calculated all of it. There is enough money being generated that you will be able to make payments, cover all costs for the business, and still make a profit. It is yours.*" I fell to the floor in tears. Let me say this one more time: I was a welfare mom. I had been on welfare for some time. Being on welfare is humiliating. You are often treated like the scum of the earth. But again, it only takes one moment to change a thousand after it.

On July 16, 2002, I became the new owner of Start To Finish Files (STFF), and it became my new legal name. I purchased the business with six locations in half the state of California, a small staff, some equipment, all the clients, and the name. Oh, that glorious name. Just like Ray Kroc, who joined McDonald's after the McDonald brothers had franchised it, I had to have that name. There is power in a name. I am everything of that name. You can be assured that whatever I start, I will finish.

I wasted no time in my pursuit to build and grow STFF. Within the first year of ownership, I expanded to Santa Barbara, California. Then, less than a year later, I expanded to Southern California with the help of my truest and most trusted employee, Joanne Jenkins. I picked up seven more locations. Business doubled, and we were booming. And just as planned, in 2004, I had fully paid off STFF and was debt-free. Imagine that. A welfare mom now a powerful CEO of her own company. Ambition!

My growth didn't stop there. I picked up more locations in Arizona and Nevada. By 2006, I was sitting at seventeen locations in three states. The work was flowing. I increased in all areas—from clients to staff to locations. It was amazing. I started to grow even more. For a number of months, work was coming in from the East Coast because there was a backlog of files that needed to be processed. California was chosen to do that work. So, Florida and Georgia were sending their work to my locations, and I was the copy service of choice, so, of course, the work came to me.

Now I had new clients, and when they started to receive the excellent customer service and reliability I gave them, they told me if I ever came to Florida or Georgia, they would make sure I had work. I said, *"Oh, is that right?"* Then, I did it. I took a big leap of faith and I expanded to the East Coast. I spent one full summer in 2007 building business in Florida and Georgia. My clients welcomed me with open arms and files galore. Work was everywhere. STFF had now grown into twenty-seven locations in five states.

"What you spend years building could be destroyed overnight; build anyways."

—Mother Teresa, missionary

That is my favorite quote by Mother Teresa. I always add that *"you never know what you are* left *with in the rubble. Perhaps a diamond in the rough, which is you."* I am that diamond, and I am that quote. After a great run, STFF slowly started declining. Can you guess why? Technology. I am a copy service. Ironically, the year I bought my business, the Social Security Administration started moving toward an electronic filing system. Paper records were going to be no more. Or, that is what we thought. There is still paper today, of course, but very little. It did take the Social Security Administration a full decade to move most of the records from paper to paperless, but nevertheless, it did take place, and it had a major impact on my thriving and growing business.

Just as Georgia and Florida starting booming, California started to decline. I had already known that paper would dissolve, even when growing my business to the East Coast. Several people questioned why I would even attempt to expand to the East Coast with the knowledge that the industry was dying. But let me ask you this question: At one point in our lives, we will give up the ghost; we will die.... Do we stop growing just because we have the knowledge of death? Absolutely not! There was money on the table, and they were telling me that it was mine for the taking. All I had to do was get up and go get it. See, it was that simple. Get up and go get what is rightfully yours. That is exactly what I did.

I had a very nice growth period while doing business in Georgia and Florida. One of the coolest parts of growing my business to the East Coast was that I had a location in my hometown of Fort Myers. That is where I was born and raised. I left there in 1996, and there I was, back home doing business—not only there, but in six other locations in Florida. I was very proud of all my hard work. Little did I realize that a flatline was coming. I mean, I knew my run wouldn't last forever, but I was certainly hoping I could last a little longer than I did. One day, it just hit. The files had dried up. Florida and Georgia were no more. Only California still had files. Nothing like before, but enough to keep me busy. I had no more employees. My equipment had changed from a copy machine to a scanner and a laptop. I was doing all I could to survive, and I was struggling emotionally. My baby, STFF, was dying.

STFF changed my entire life. It took me from welfare to wealth, and it was looking like I might be heading back to welfare. I continued to do all I could to stay in the game. I started scanning records, specifically closed records, and to this day, I still scan for one of my longest-standing clients, Patrick Kelly. I have been scanning his records for a very long time. He is my faithful client, and I am so grateful for him. Scanning, however, didn't last that long because the economy crashed. When it did, even those with money held on to the change they had. It was dark times for our country and our people. Secondly, scanners started becoming more accessible and more user-friendly. So, again, out went the middleman, and the internal staff was given the task to handle scanning.

In Social Security disability law, there are court reporters called "verbatim hearing monitors." They use a keyboard and a recording system to document the disability hearing. They are contract workers. Many of my clients recommended that I try to bid on one of the contracts, and that was exactly what I did. The first time I put in a bid on the contract, they closed it without hiring any contractors. Some funding issues came up. I continued to watch for it, and it opened again. By this time, I was attending California State University, pursuing my master's degree in business administration. I was almost done, and I thought of how great it would be to transition from graduate school into a new season with STFF.

I placed a bid on a contract to be a verbatim hearing monitor and won sixteen federal contracts in the state of California. The contract was worth up to $1.5 million over a five-year period. Because my copy service was so well-known for superior customer service and reliability, it was an easy win. Shortly after, I graduated with my master's and gave birth to my daughter. I started working as a clerk, mainly in Sacramento, San Rafael, and San Francisco, and held open contracts in other locations.

Clerking was interesting but short-lived. In Sacramento, I had a judge who thought I was too big to be in his presence. I have struggled with my weight most of my life due to the intense amount of trauma I have endured. I had just given birth to my daughter and had gone through one of the most painful events of my life. I pretty much lost my business, my home that I lived in for almost a decade, and damn near my mind. I was carrying a lot of weight— physically, mentally, and emotionally. But it was the physical weight you could see, and he didn't like that I was a heavy-set woman.

The Social Security Administration tried to take away all my locations, but my judges in other offices came to my rescue and spoke on behalf of my work ethic and character. I was able to keep everything but Sacramento. This, however, made it increasingly hard for me to work, as I now had to travel several hours to earn money. But I did what I needed to do. I clerked for almost two years. Then, the Social Security Administration decided they were going to pause the contracts and have in-house staff do the clerking. It was a big mess and it didn't last very long, but by that point, I had moved on.

While I was clerking, I learned more and more about Social Security disability law. My judges encouraged me to practice law. In Social Security disability law, you can practice as an attorney or as a non-attorney. As a non-attorney, you can be paid just as much as an attorney if you pass the test given by the federal government. I had both attorneys and non-attorneys as my clients, so I was aware that there were two different types, but I didn't know much more than that. I told some of my closest clients that I was considering working as a non-attorney. They were all very supportive. I began to study the Code of Federal Regulations—parts 400 to 499. I paid to take the test and flew myself to Baltimore. I passed. I had now become my own client and spin-off of STFF. And STFF Disability Advocacy Group was born.

I did some work for another non-attorney and I won the case, but she felt like I didn't deserve to receive the monetary split, which was $6,000. At that point, I was done. I wanted nothing more to do with Social Security disability law. I decided not to practice, and I turned my attention to pursuing teaching. One of the main reasons I earned my master's degree was to teach at the college level. I had always wanted to be a teacher. As I said earlier, prior to buying and taking ownership of my business, I was going to school to be a high school photography teacher. I had been a guest teacher and speaker ever since I graduated with my bachelor's degree.

I was shifting so fast at this point, and I was struggling financially. I had to stabilize my financial health. I still had STFF, but there was very little work—certainly not enough to live off of. The contracts were gone, and I was not practicing. I started applying for state jobs and was hired by the State of California Department of Transportation. It was the worst eighteen months of my life. I was never built to be a nine-to-five worker. I am a workhorse who will work around the clock—I am an Empowered Entrepreneur, damn it. During the same time that I applied for state jobs, I also applied for the faculty diversity internship with Los Rios Community College District. I had found out about the program a year prior but missed the application deadline by three days. When it opened again, I was ready. My application was accepted, and I was selected for an interview. Mind you, I'm a pretty polished educator, but at that time, I was nervous. In the teaching demo, I failed to state my name. One could see my nerves, I'm sure. I can still remember walking out of my new state job office with my cell phone in my hand, reading the email from Los Rios telling me that I was not selected for the internship. I was crushed. I called my son and just cried. He said, *"Mom, one blessing at a time. You just got the state job; it is not time for the internship. It doesn't mean it won't happen. It just means it wasn't going to happen this year."*

Oh, the wisdom of our youth. He was right. One blessing at a time. I was able to stabilize by working the state job, and my financial health recovered. Then, a year passed, and the faculty diversity internship opened again. You already know what I did. I applied! The application and all supporting documents were ready to go. I was selected for an interview, and trust and believe me, I was not going to forget my name this time. I went into the interview with full confidence. I knocked the teaching demo out of the park. I remember telling Dolly, my interviewer, that I had been waiting for this moment for three years. I explained how I found out about the internship three years prior, but the application had closed three days prior to finding out. Then I explained that the next year I was selected for an interview but forgot to say my name. She said, *"You have waited three years for this?" "Yes, ma'am,"* I replied, *"and hopefully the wait is now over."*

It was just a little over three weeks later that the congratulatory email came in. I was elated. I mean, beaming with joy and bursting at my seams with excitement! One moment changes a thousand after it. You remember me telling you that, right? This was that one moment, yet again. I started the internship in the fall of 2014. We had eight weeks of coursework. We met once every Saturday. Then, in the spring of 2015, we were able to co-teach.

Now I told you I hated the state job, so I left it. I left in about the second week of November 2014. I was just starting my internship with Los Rios and I already knew that being a professor is what I would be doing, and no matter what, I would be fine. God was with me. He had never failed me, and He would not now. Leap of faith once again. (You will see this is a theme for me.)

There I was, no longer surviving but rather thriving. I was glowing on a daily basis. The internship validated that, indeed, being a college professor was one of the callings in my life. The coolest part about the internship was that I was able to co-teach at Sacramento City College. That was the college I attended and where I earned my associate's degree in photography. I had come full circle. I was giving back, which I love to do. I have used education as the foundation of a better life, and today it serves as the scaffold to building the life I have always dreamed of having. Sacramento City College was where my metamorphosis began in 1998. Now I was back, and I was reaching the student body I once was a part of. It was empowering, to say the least.

After the internship, I hit the ground running. I was grinding and grinding in pursuit of a teaching job. Finally, in the spring of 2016, I was hired at Sierra College. I was hired to teach one class in the fall of 2016—Business 20: Introduction to Business. Right before the fall of 2016 began, my department chair reached out and told me she had not just one more class, but two additional classes for me to teach. One more Business 20, and Business 140: Small Business Management and Entrepreneurship.

I was floored. It was all I could do to contain myself. I had been told NO for so long and so many times that—truth be told—I was slowly losing heart. But I am gritty. I never give up on my goals and dreams. I understood a very powerful principle that I will share with you now:

"You have RIGHTS to your NO, and your YES is UNDENIABLE!"

—Natasha M Palumbo, author and educator

I need all of you to understand this valuable Palumbo Principle. Your YES is far more powerful and purposeful than any NO you will ever receive. My YES is seven figures, eight when I leave this earth. My YES is speaking to seas upon seas of people in many nations. My YES is 6'4" and fine, and when he finally arrives, he will be right on time. The dice of life will throw you a NO time and time again. I want you to pick those dice up, shake them in your hand, spit on them if you need to, and throw them back to the world and, with everything you have inside you, say, "MY YES IS UNDENIABLE!"

Today, I not only work at one community college, but four—and one state university. I inspire classrooms full of students, and when they leave me, they leave *EMPOWERED* with the keys to their life. I have given them the gift of their authentic selves, which is the greatest gift of all. Being an Empowered Entrepreneur is just a bonus. They get that, too, but it's nothing compared to the gift of self with no shame, freedom to live in their rightful place in the world, and, most importantly, to be matrix-free.

I have shared with you the core of my entrepreneurial journey to date, but I didn't tell you everything. I am a serial entrepreneur. I have owned other businesses, and I am still building new ones to this day. I have had a photography business for a little longer than I have had STFF, but it has been more of a love than a business. I have made a nice sum of money doing it, and I still work on it today. I love it more than anything, and if you know any artist, they are normally starving, but I was much wiser. I have used it as a residual income source, and today it remains. I first started the business as Ldy Bug Images. Today, I use my name: Natasha Palumbo Professional Photography. Most of my work comes via word of mouth. I promise you that word of mouth is your best marketing tool around. It is how I grew STFF, as well as my photography business.

In 2005, I purchased a tanning salon because, well, I just simply didn't already have enough to do. My salon was called Italian Tans. It had a short run of just slightly over a year. I did very well in the business and had just over 300 clients come through my doors, but it was connected to a gym that was a money pit, and I could no longer do it. I had to close the doors. I sold all my beds, furniture, and mirrors. I had one stand-up bed that I had bought for $300.00.... I flipped it for $3,000. You can do the math on that one. That was lovely. I made really good money on liquidating all the equipment and the like. Then, I moved forward and focused my attention on STFF and Ldy Bug Images.

Due to all the experience I had, which now is expertise, I launched a consulting firm in 2010 and started working with small business owners one-on-one. I help analyze and correct organizational matters, review financial records in the pursuit of cash flow efficiencies and increased financial health, design and deliver trainings, and create systems and set them in place. I work with top management and provide them with my time and talents as they are needed. I have saved my clients hundreds of thousands of dollars, which they were able to return to their business and use for future growth. I have been instrumental in saving many small businesses that were failing due to their owner's lack of knowledge and skills. I still work as a business consultant and meet with clients on a regular basis. From start-up to succession, I work with them at all levels.

Finally, I have been serving the homeless since 2004. My organization is called the STEEL Legacy, which stands for *Serve, Teach, Encourage, Empower, and Lead.* This is my heart. I told you earlier, I love to give back. I will always extend my time and talents to those whom society has deemed unimportant. I have an outreach once every quarter. The fall outreach is normally held between October and November. It is dedicated to providing a full meal, along with other items, such as socks or rain gear. The winter outreach is held between December and January. It is dedicated to keeping the homeless warm. Did you know the homeless actually freeze to death? Yet, churches go empty Monday through Saturday. (I'll leave that one alone, though.) The spring outreach is held between March and April. It is dedicated to hygiene. The summer outreach is dedicated to keeping cool, sunblock, and water. All the water we can get. Cold water. Just as the homeless die from the cold, they also die from the heat.

At every outreach, we provide some type of food. We also provide small first aid kits. My thought is, if I can help them with a small wound they have on their body, they may not get so sick inside. We also make sure to provide water in every outreach. I wish I could say that each year we serve fewer and fewer people who are homeless, but that is not the case. We increase. Homelessness is an epidemic directly tied to mental health. It will require intense work to be fully cured—if ever.

Now you have been introduced to Start To Finish Files (STFF), Ldy Bug Images, Italian Tans, and the STEEL Legacy, but more importantly, to Natasha M Palumbo, the LION who runs the jungle. Today, I am in the business of building up people who build businesses. I call them my students and clients. I deliver to them the keys of freedom, equipping them with the tools, resources, and even possible opportunities for funding to make their business dreams come true.

My journey in academia has been interesting, to say the least. What I have found is that the books are subpar, and many textbooks are overpriced. I finally found my students a free online book, which I somewhat like, but it is dated. My goal from the moment I started my journey in pursuit of becoming a professor was to always be able to bring my students, and really any audience I could get my hands on, the most current, up-to-date information available. I will always share the truth of business. Not what the textbooks want to tell you, but rather what my life experience has been. What I know works—what real Empowered Entrepreneurs are doing, and what real investors are looking for.

As you have seen thus far, I have been a very successful businesswoman. I bent the arch of sexism, and I owned the company. I have ambition, and I believe you do, too. I am Professor Palumbo, your new millennium professor.

Business Legal Structures

Because the business structures are perplexing, I have defined them again for you below. These definitions come directly from the SBA.

"A **sole proprietorship** is a business that is owned and usually operated by one person. It is the oldest, simplest, and cheapest form of business ownership because there is no legal distinction made between the owner and the business.

A **partnership** is two or more people voluntarily operating a business as co-owners for profit. Partnerships make up more than 8 percent of all businesses in the United States and more than 11 percent of the total revenue.

A **C corporation** is an artificial person created by law, with most of the legal rights of a real person. These include the rights to start and operate a business, to buy or sell property, to borrow money, to sue or be sued, and to enter into binding contracts. Corporations make up 20 percent of all businesses in the United States, but they account for almost 90 percent of the revenue.

S corporations are corporations that elect to pass corporate income, losses, deductions, and credits through to their shareholders for federal tax purposes. Shareholders of S corporations report the flow-through of income and losses on their personal tax returns and are assessed tax at their individual income tax rates. This allows S corporations to avoid double taxation on the corporate income. S corporations are responsible for tax on certain built-in gains and passive income at the entity level.

The limited liability company is a relatively new form of business ownership that is now permitted in all fifty states, although the laws of each state may differ. The LLC is a blend of a sole proprietorship and a corporation: the owners of the LLC have limited liability and are taxed only once for the business."[4]

Now for the legal business structures that must have some type of social endeavor: ***Low-Profit Limited Liability Company***, also known as **L3C**. *"A low-profit limited liability company (L3C) is a legal form of business entity in the United States that was created to bridge the gap between non-profit and for-profit investing by providing a structure that facilitates investments in socially beneficial, for-profit ventures by simplifying compliance with Internal Revenue Service rules for program-related investments, a type of investment that private foundations are allowed to make."*

The following information comes from the SBA. *"**B corp.** A benefit corporation, sometimes called a B corp, is a for-profit corporation recognized in the majority of U.S. states. B corps are different from C corps in purpose, accountability, and transparency, but aren't different in how they're taxed. B corps are driven by both mission and profit.*

Nonprofit corporation. *Nonprofit corporations are organized to do charity, education, religious, literary, or scientific work. Because their work benefits the public, nonprofits can receive tax-exempt status, meaning they don't pay state or federal taxes income taxes on any profits they make."*[14]

Business Structure	Ownership	Liability	Taxes
Sole Proprietor	One Person	Unlimited Personal Liability	Personal Tax Only
Partnerships	Two or More People	Unlimited Personal Liability Unless Structured as a Limited Partnership	Self-Employment Tax (except for limited partnerships) Personal Tax
Limited Liability Company (LLC)	One or More People	Owners Are Not Personally Liable	Self-Employment Tax Personal Tax or Corporate Tax
Corporation C – Corp	One or More People	Owners Are Not Personally Liable	Corporate Tax
Corporation S – Corp	One or More People, But No More Than 100, and all must be U.S. Citizens	Owners Are Not Personally Liable	Personal Tax
Corporation B – Corp	One or More People	Owners Are Not Personally Liable	Corporate Tax
Corporation Nonprofit	One or More People	Owners Are Not Personally Liable	Tax-Exempt, But Corporate Profits Can't be Distributed

Created by Entrepreneurship Empowered, based on information from SBA: Business Legal Structures

Business Plan Template

The following information comes directly from the SBA and is the more formal business plan template.

- "*Executive summary*
    - *Briefly tell your reader what your company is and why it will be successful. Include your mission statement, your product or service, and basic information about your company's leadership team, employees, and location. You should also include financial information and high-level growth plans if you plan to ask for financing.*
- *Company description*
    - *Use your company description to provide detailed information about your company. Go into detail about the problems your business solves. Be specific, and list out the consumers, organization, or businesses your company plans to serve.*
    - *Explain the competitive advantages that will make your business a success. Are there experts on your team? Have you found the perfect location for your store? Your company description is the place to boast about your strengths.*
- *Market analysis*
    - *You'll need a good understanding of your industry outlook and target market. Competitive research will show you what other businesses are doing and what their strengths are. In your market research, look for trends and themes. What do successful competitors do? Why does it work? Can you do it better? Now's the time to answer these questions.*
- *Organization and management*
    - *Tell your reader how your company will be structured and who will run it.*
    - *Describe the legal structure of your business. State whether you have or intend to incorporate your business as a C or an S corporation; form a general or limited partnership; or if you're a sole proprietor or LLC.*
    - *Use an organizational chart to lay out who's in charge of what in your company. Show how each person's unique experience will*

contribute to the success of your venture. Consider including résumés and CV's of key members of your team.

- ***Service or product line***
    - *Describe what you sell or what service you offer. Explain how it benefits your customers and what the product lifecycle looks like. Share your plans for intellectual property, like copyright or patent filings. If you're doing research and development for your service or product, explain it in detail.*
- ***Marketing and sales***
    - *There's no single way to approach a marketing strategy. Your strategy should evolve and change to fit your unique needs.*
    - *Your goal in this section is to describe how you'll attract and retain customers. You'll also describe how a sale will actually happen. You'll refer to this section later when you make financial projections, so make sure to thoroughly describe your complete marketing and sales strategies.*
- ***Funding request***
    - *If you're asking for funding, this is where you'll outline your funding requirements. Your goal is to clearly explain how much funding you'll need over the next five years and what you'll use it for.*
    - *Specify whether you want debt or equity, the terms you'd like applied, and the length of time your request will cover. Give a detailed description of how you'll use your funds. Specify if you need funds to buy equipment or materials, pay salaries, or cover specific bills until revenue increases. Always include a description of your future strategic financial plans, like paying off debt or selling your business.*
- ***Financial projections***
    - *Supplement your funding request with financial projections. Your goal is to convince the reader that your business is stable and will be a financial success.*
    - *If your business is already established, include income statements, balance sheets, and cash flow statements for the last three to five years. If you have other collateral you could put against a loan, make sure to list it now.*
    - *Provide a prospective financial outlook for the next five years. Include forecasted income statements, balance sheets, cash flow statements, and capital expenditure budgets. For the first year, be even more specific and use quarterly—or even monthly—*

projections. Make sure to clearly explain your projections and match them to your funding requests.
- *o This is a great place to use graphs and charts to tell the financial story of your business.*
- **Appendix**
  - *o Use your appendix to provide supporting documents or other materials were specially requested. Common items to include are credit histories, résumés, product pictures, letters of reference, licenses, permits, patents legal documents, permits, and other contracts."*[14]

Marketing Plan

The following information is from the SBA and is the most common marketing template.

- *"Target market*
  - *Describe your audience in detail. Look at the market's size, demographics, unique traits, and trends that relate to demand for your business.*
- *Competitive advantage*
  - *Describe what gives your product or service an advantage over the competition. It might be a better product, a lower price, or an excellent customer experience. Sometimes, an environmentally friendly certification or "made in the USA" on your label can be an important factor for customers.*
- *Sales plan*
  - *Describe how you'll literally sell your service or product to your customers. List the sales methods you'll use, like retail, wholesale, or your own online store. Explain each step your customer takes once they decide to buy.*
- *Marketing and sales goals*
  - *Describe your marketing and sales goals for the next year. Common marketing and sales goals are to increase email subscribers, grow market share, or increase sales by a certain percent.*
- *Marketing action plan*
  - *Describe how you'll achieve your marketing and sales goals. List marketing channels you'll use, like online advertising, radio ads, or billboards. Explain your pricing strategy and how you'll use promotions. Talk about the customer support that happens after the sale. The federal government regulates advertising and labeling for a number of consumer products, so make sure your advertising is legally compliant.*
- *Budget*
  - *Include a complete breakdown of the costs of your marketing plan. Try to be as accurate as possible. You'll want to keep tracking your costs once you put your plan into action."*[14]

Income Statement, Balance Sheet, and Cash Flow

Entrepreneurship Empowered
Income Statement Model
January 1 through December 31, 20____

Net Sales	$725,425	
Less: Cost of Goods Sold	456,740	
Gross Income		$268,685
Operating Expenses:		
Salaries	$125,698	
Utilities	8,689	
Depreciation	15,025	
Rent	3,500	
Building Services	5,985	
Insurance	6,200	
Interest	2,585	
Office Supplies	13,259	
Sales Promotion	16,120	
Taxes and Licenses	6,848	
Maintenance	1,258	
Delivery	3,895	
Miscellaneous	1,125	
Total Expenses		$210,187
Net Income Before Taxes		58,498
Less: Income Taxes		14,624
Net Income After Taxes		43,874

Entrepreneurship Empowered
Balance Sheet Model
December 31, 20____

Assets

Current Assets:		
Cash	$ 8,758	
Accounts Receivable	61,984	
Inventory	82,054	
Prepaid Expenses	1,650	
Total Current Assets		$154,446
Fixed Assets:		
Equipment	$100,750	
Building	54,965	
Gross Fixed Assets	$155,715	
Less Accumulated Depreciation	19,985	
Net Fixed Assets		138,730
Total Assets		$293,176

Liabilities and Owners Equity

Current Liabilities:		
Accounts Payable	$62,482	
Accrued Payable	4,640	
Total Current Liabilities		$67,122
Long – Term Liabilities:		
Mortgage Payable		32,680
Total Liabilities		$ 99,802
Owners' Equity:		
Capital Stock	165,000	
Retained Earnings	28,374	
Total Equity		193,374
Total Liabilities and Owners Equity		$293,176

Entrepreneurship Empowered
Cash Flow Statement Model
For the Year Ended December 31, 20____

Cash Flow From Operations

Net Income………………………………………………..	89,500
Adjustments for depreciation…………………………..	2,500
Adjustments for increased inventories…………………	(25,000)
Adjustments for decrease in accounts receivable…….	13,000
Net Cash Flow from Operations………………………..	68,300

Cash Flow from Investing

Cash receipts from sale of property and equipment….	12,000
Cash paid for purchase of equipment…………………	(14,000)
Net Cash Flow from Investing………………………….	(2,000)

Cash Flow from Financing

Cash paid for loan repayment…………………………	(6,500)
Net Cash Flow from Financing………………………..	(6,500)

Net Increase in Cash   59,800

Accounting Terms & Definitions

Terms and definitions as defined by the dictionary:

Revenue: the value received by a firm in return for a good or service.
Expenses: the costs of labor, goods, and services.
Cost of goods sold: the total cost in terms of raw materials, labor, and overhead of the business that can be allocated to production.
Net income: the total revenue in an accounting period minus all expenses during the same period. If income taxes and interest are not deducted, it is called operating profit (or loss, as the case may be).
Assets: the things a business owns, includes cash, accounts receivable, inventory, equipment, building.
Current assets: cash and other assets that are expected to be converted to cash within a year.
Fixed assets: is a long-term tangible piece of property that a firm owns and uses in its operations to generate income. Fixed assets take longer than a year to convert to cash.
Accounts receivable: current assets resulting from selling a product on credit.
Goodwill (not the store): is a long-term (or noncurrent) asset categorized as an intangible asset.
Intangible assets: is an asset that is not physical in nature. Goodwill, brand recognition and intellectual property, such as patents, trademarks and copyrights, are all intangible assets.
Long-term investments: is an account on the asset side of a company's balance sheet that represents the company's investments, including stocks, bonds, real estate and cash that it intends to hold for more than a year.
Liabilities: is defined as a company's legal financial debts or obligations that arise during the course of business operations.
Current liabilities: are debts payable within one year.
Accounts payable: money owed by a company to its creditors.
Accrued expenses: are payments that a company is obligated to pay in the future for which goods and services have already been delivered.
Short-term debt: is an account shown in the current liabilities portion of a company's balance sheet. This account is made up of any debt incurred by a company that is due within one year.

Long-term debt: consists of loans and financial obligations lasting over one year. Long-term debt for a company would include any financing or leasing obligations that are to come due after a 12-month period.

Shareholder equity: also referred to as the owner's residual claim after debts have been paid, is equal to a firm's total assets minus its total liabilities.

Retained earnings: are the profits that a company has earned to date, less any dividends or other distributions paid to investors.

Capital stock: is the number of common and preferred shares that a company is authorized to issue, according to its corporate charter.

Answer Key

Kid Tested. Mother Approved.
Life's Good
Trusted Everywhere
Maybe She's Born With It
We Try Harder
Keep Walking
Gather 'Round the Good Stuff
Makes Mouths Happy
Something Special in the Air
It's Not Just a Job, It's an Adventure!

Kix Cereal — The famous low sugar, round cereal!
LG Electronics — LG manufactures high quality flat panel televisions.
Duracell Batteries — Called "The Coppertop"
Maybelline — Maybelline was started in 1915!
Avis — Avis is headquartered in Parsippany, New Jersey.
Johnnie Walker — Johnnie Walker Scotch Whiskey is produced in Scotland.
Pizza Hut — Pizza Hut is owned by the same company that owns Taco Bell.
Twizzlers — Twizzlers flavors include chocolate, strawberry, and watermelon.
American Airlines — American Airlines is headquartered in Ft. Worth, Texas.
Navy — The Department of the Navy is a division of the Department of Defense.

References and Resources

Anthony Grigsby (Business Insurance agent)
110 N San Joaquin St
2nd FL #31
Stockton, CA 95202
(P) 209-888-4904
(F) 209-888-5094
www.worldeventsinsurance.com
CA Lic.# 0G50664

1 Daniel, C. "The 4 Animals Assessment." (n.d.). The 4 Animals Experience. Accessed December 20, 2020.
   https://4animalsassessment.com/page-29740388.

2 VARK Questionnaire:
   http://vark-learn.com/the-vark-questionnaire/.

3 The 5 Love Languages Questionnaire:
   https://www.5lovelanguages.com/quizzes/

4 Duckworth, A.L., Peterson, C., Matthews, M.D., and Kelly, D.R. (2007). Grit: Perseverance and Passion for Long-Term Goals. *Journal of Personality and Social Psychology.* Vol. 92. 1087–1101.

5 Virtue, Doreen. (2015.) *Don't Let Anything Dull Your Sparkle: How to Break Free of Negativity and Drama.* Hay House, INC.

6 "Personal Efficiency and Effectiveness." (n.d.) *Modern Management of Small Business.* Vol. 1.0. Accessed January 7, 2021.
   https://2012books.lardbucket.org/books/modern-management-of-small-businesses/s17-01-personal-efficiency-and-effect.html.

7 Watt, Adrienne. (2014.) *Project Management.* Accessed January 7, 2021.
   https://opentextbc.ca/projectmanagement/chapter/chapter-3-the-project-life-cycle-phases-project-management/

8 Project Management blog. (n.d.) Project Manager. Accessed January 7, 2021.
https://www.projectmanager.com/blog/project-management-for-startups-entrepreneurs

9 Project Plan blog. (n.d.) Project Manager. Accessed January 7, 2021.
https://www.projectmanager.com/academy/how-to-make-a-project-plan.

10 Swanbrow, Diane. (2010.) "Empathy: College Students Don't Have as Much as They Used To." University of Michigan News. Accessed January 7, 2021.
https://news.umich.edu/empathy-college-students-don-t-have-as-much-as-they-used-to/.

11 IDEO "Design Thinking." (n.d.) Accessed January 7, 2021.
https://designthinking.ideo.com/faq/whats-the-difference-between-human-centered-design-and-design-thinking/.

12 IDEO website:
https://www.ideo.org/.

13 "What Is Human-Centered Design?" (n.d.) DC Design. Accessed January 7, 2021.
https://medium.com/dc-design/what-is-human-centered-design-6711c09e2779.

14 Small Business Administration (SBA) website:
https://www.sba.gov/.

15 Nolo website:
https://www.nolo.com/.

16 United States Patent and Trademark Office website:
https://www.uspto.gov/.

17 Internal Revenue Service website:
https://www.irs.gov/.

18 "What is a Pitch Deck? (And How to Make One.)" (n.d.) Design Shack. Accessed January 7, 2021.
https://designshack.net/articles/business-articles/what-is-a-pitch-deck/.

19 Mehrabain, Albert. (1971.) *Silent Messages: Implicit Communication of Emotions and Attitudes.* Wadsworth Publishing Company.

20 Giang, Vivian. (2014.) "7 Email Etiquette Rules Every Professional Should Know." Accessed January 7, 2021.
   https://www.careerbuilder.com/advice/seven-email-etiquette-rules-every-professional-should-know.

21 O'Hara, Carolyn. (2014.) "How to Improve Your Business Writing." Harvard Business Review. Accessed January 12, 2020.
   https://hbr.org/2014/11/how-to-improve-your-business-writing.

22 Przybyla, Dena. (n.d.) "The Psychology of Colors in Marketing and Branding." Accessed January 30, 2020.
   https://www.colorpsychology.org/color-psychology-marketing/.

23 Berger, Jonah. (2016.) *Contagious: Why Things Catch On.* Published by Simon & Schuster. New York: New York.

24 Active Marketing website:
   https://www.activemarketing.com/our-work/.

25 Cooper, Paige. (2020.) "20 LinkedIn Statistics That Matter to Marketers in 2020." Hootsuite. Accessed January 7, 2021.
   https://blog.hootsuite.com/linkedin-statistics-business/.

26 Facebook Statistics. Accessed December 8, 2020.
   https://www.oberlo.com/blog/facebookstatistics

27 Uzzi, Brian and Shannon Dunlap. (2005.) "How to Build Your Network." *Harvard Business Review*. Accessed January 7, 2021.
   https://hbr.org/2005/12/how-to-build-your-nework#:~:text=According%20to%20our%20studies%2C%20if,network%20may%20be%20too%20inbred.

28 Kenton, Will. (2020.) "Human Capital." Investopedia. Accessed January 7, 2021.
   https://www.investopedia.com/terms/h/humancapital.asp#:~:text=Human%20capital%20is%20an%20intangible,such%20as%20loyalty%20and%20punctuality.

29 Workable website:
   https://www.workable.com/.

30 Ou, Amy Y., Waldman, David A., and Peterson, Suzanne J. (2015.) "Do Humble CEOs Matter?" *Journal of Management.* Accessed January 7, 2021.
    https://createvalue.org/wp-content/uploads/Do-Humble-CEOs-Matter.pdf.

31 Glazer, Robert. (2018.) "How Training Like a Pilot Will Set You Up for Success." *Forbes.* Accessed January 7, 2021.
    https://www.forbes.com/sites/robertglazer/2018/07/13/how-training-like-a-pilot-will-set-you-up-for-success-in-crisis-management/#62059d1f7dde.

32 "What is Transformational Leadership? How New Ideas Produce Impressive Results." (2014.) STU online. Accessed January 7, 2021.
    https://online.stu.edu/articles/education/what-is-transformational-leadership.aspx.

33 Dun & Bradstreet website:
    https://www.dnb.com.

34 Kumar, Vineet. (2014.) "Making 'Freemium' Work." *Harvard Business Review.* Accessed January 7, 2021.
    https://hbr.org/2014/05/making-freemium-work.

35 Reiff, Nathan. (2020.) "Series A, B, C Funding: How It Works." Investopedia. Accessed January 7, 2021.
    https://www.investopedia.com/articles/personal-finance/102015/series-b-c-funding-what-it-all-means-and-how-it-works.asp

About the Author

Ms. Palumbo is a business professional with more than 20 years of experience, 18 as an entrepreneur. She is a creative leader with in-depth knowledge and expertise applying strategic business management, development of small business initiatives, and progressive leadership. Ms. Palumbo is an effective communicator with an innate ability to engage and hold the attention of those she trains and teaches. She owns several businesses, and she successfully grew her core business into multiple states. She is a social entrepreneur and has been serving the homeless community for more than 17 years. In addition to being an Empowered Entrepreneur, Ms. Palumbo is a Business Adjunct professor for several colleges in the greater Sacramento region.

Natasha M Palumbo, MBA
Author, Coach, Consultant and Speaker
Entrepreneur – Educator – Empowered

Instagram and LinkedIn: Natasha M Palumbo
natasha@natashapalumbo.com